UNZIP MY SKIN
A COLLECTION OF REFLECTIVE ESSAYS

By

Tsitsi Michelle Zawaira

Copyright Page
Unzip my Skin

© 2025 Tsitsi M. Zawaira
All rights reserved.

No part of this book may be reproduced, distributed, or transmitted in any form or by any means, including photocopying, recording, or other electronic or mechanical methods, without the prior written permission of the author or publisher, except in the case of brief quotations embodied in critical reviews and certain other noncommercial uses permitted by copyright law.

This is a work of nonfiction (or fiction). Names, characters, businesses, places, events, and incidents are either the products of the author's imagination or used in a fictitious manner. Any resemblance to actual persons, living or dead, or actual events is purely coincidental.

Published by Tsitsi M. Zawaira [Unbowed Spirit] Minneapolis, MN

ISBN: 979-8-218-58492-4

Cover design by Tsitsi M. Zawaira.
Developed in collaboration with AI-powered tools. Interior design and formatting by Tsitsi M. Zawaira

For permissions, please contact: www.unbowedspirit.com

First Edition: 01/2025

Dedication

To my nieces and nephews (my children),
I love you so very much. It is your future that
keeps me loving, believing and hoping.

TABLE OF CONTENTS

Preface	1
Introduction	8

Chapters:
1. What do they call me? – "Masivanda"	16
2. Unzip my Skin	23
3. Being each other's missing piece and peace	31
4. Deciphering the Fragmented Collective Soul	41
5. The wound that awakened Joy	58
6. Navigating the Middle Passage: the inner journey from "there" to "here"	72
7. Unmasking the complexities of Spiritual Violence	80
8. Erasure's echo	89
9. African Hair/Black Hair: My perspective	96
10. It is almost always about Respect	105
11. The Power in reclaiming a Question	117
Epilogue - "The day I saw Her"	129
Acknowledgments	147
References/ Works Cited	149

PREFACE

"Who are your people? Where are your people from?". These are common questions Afro descendants all over the world ask each other as a way to establish a connection or common ground. I am what they call a continental African. That is an African born and raised on the continent of Africa (and in my case, Zimbabwe). The aforementioned questions became a cornerstone of my experience as an immigrant in America. They helped me redefine and reclaim my Power because everything I thought I knew about the history of Afro peoples was turned upside down. The more I learned about the life of Black people in the United States (past and present) and all over the diaspora, the more I felt both spiritually expanded and exhausted.

By the time I was compiling my essays for this book, I had lived outside of Zimbabwe and inside America for almost an equal amount of time. I had lived outside the African continent long enough to not be considered "African/Zimbabwean enough" anymore by some. On the other hand, I was not really seen or accepted as "Black enough" either in the US, ever since I had arrived here. It is important to note that I neither denied nor pandered to be seen and accepted as either of these identities. Nope. In fact, it became a growing awareness that I was either a statement or an action away from getting both my African or Black card revoked, which was a bizarrely freeing state of existence.

This state of being, a state of "statelessness" as it were, granted me a gift. One that I initially resented to be quite honest. Until one day I finally saw the purpose of being "stateless". Being "stateless" gifted me an unfettered opportunity to examine what African-ness and/or Blackness means to me. Not what colonization tried to erase or replace with a new version of history that I studied in grade school. Not what the adults in Zimbabwean society decided to force-feed or withhold using the culture of silence. Not what the experience of being an immigrant in America attempted to silence and erase within my soul. Not what the ideology of whiteness vis à vis political correctness threatened to deny or dismiss about being an Afro descendant. I had the chance to question everything. To do so without the fear of betraying the personality that had been bestowed upon me and that I had also created thus far in my life. I was led by the liberating pain of disillusionment as well as the pure audacity of who I once was as a child. I asked questions with curious wonderment, some got answered whilst others remained lingering in sight. I am still, to this day, in a continual conversation with some recurring themes that you will observe in this book, all born out of the main concept called Power.

Power manifested itself as sub-concepts that include pride, home, respect and a few more, which all stood out as I was awakening. I thoroughly enjoyed the excavation that came with these concepts because the journey was anchored by the following profoundly healing notion. Quick story: on one of my meditative walks, I arrived at my prayer spot and started to lament to God as well as my ancestors. I was asking for guidance and a path forward from the stuck-ness I felt because of the statelessness I mentioned earlier. As I was listing the names of the ancestors I was calling on, it became glaringly clear to me at that moment that none of them were African American. And just like that, for as long as I had lived in

America, I uncovered a heartbreak that was masquerading as a thought. I thought I couldn't claim my Afro descendant ancestors who had been taken off the continent of Africa and placed in different parts of the world. In my case, American ancestors of Afro descent.

The rift that was and is imprinted in African History through colonization and slavery led me to believe this rather destructive lie. I cried uncontrollably during that prayer. It stopped being about the requests I was making and turned into a grieving session. Unbeknownst to me the destructive lie, this seemingly invisible and painful ache I had lived with for a while was exposed, and the process of true healing began. I didn't know it when I landed in America years back, but a piece of ME was being reintroduced back to myself the moment I stepped foot on American soil.

Herein lies the healing notion: in order to traverse the minefield that is African-ness and/or Blackness in the American context, I needed guidance from those who knew the landscape of the country I now resided. And there it was, I finally asked them, and they answered back. The ancestors who lived and died on this American soil awakened me to who they were and are, as MY people. And ultimately awakened me to who I AM. Whenever I need strength and wisdom, I call upon them for fortification, I call upon them to lead me Home. I have been called to embrace the shared heritage of Afro descendants and give voice to the fragmented stories within our collective story worldwide. I unearthed a kind of healing strength the moment I honored my ancestors (both on the continental and in the diaspora) and uncovered an unbowed sense of Self within me.

A Self not bound by geographic proximity to the African continent or by the romanticization of it either. A Self not bound by the sexualization and infantilization of the Black body as well as the Black mind. A Self that does not deny both regionalistic and nationalistic sensibilities but can think beyond them. A Self that recognizes and flourishes within its individual expression without demeaning, denying or dismissing the collective Afro identity. At the behest of the many ancestors and living elders, I followed my path to healing because my life really does depend on it. The quote I share with you below is from one such ancestor. It has served as my guiding light through this beautiful minefield.

"It took many years of vomiting up all the filth I'd been taught about myself, and half believed before I was able to walk on earth as though I had the right to be here." - James Baldwin

Important Sidenote:

Throughout this book, I will be using the words 'God' and 'Creator' interchangeably. I speak of healing through a spiritual vantage point which is neither about religious theology per se nor is it about a particular religion. These names represent the infinite power that has loved me my entire life. I believe that this power is a source of love which dwells within everything and is everything. I honor those who have their own understanding of these words.

I honor those who are currently waking up to their own spirituality and the wounds that may have come from past experiences with religion. I honor those who have found whatever spiritual practices that anchor them, evolve them and truly aligns them - those who have released performative goodness. I honor those who are open and willing to respect that which is sacred and real to me regarding these words.

There are many words and/or phrases that deserve a thorough re-examination of our relationship with them. I did my spiritual re-examination, and this book is a partial inside look into what resulted from my healing expedition. It is imperative I say that I still derive reverence, protection, enthusiasm and love from using the words 'God' and

'Creator'. I can only urge you to choose to be a witness to this book, for as long as you are willing. And hopefully using what you read to help either assuage or encourage you to do more investigation into any resistance that comes up for you. May your curiosity about yourself guide the parts of you that are willing to heal. Remember, this book isn't about offending you, even if you may experience some offense. I know that is a difficult concept to grasp when you live in a culture that is addicted to civilizing and un-civilizing others.

My hope is that you will try anyway.

INTRODUCTION

Black Implosions. That is what it felt like when I was writing these essays. Exploring, examining, excavating how I've worn this African skin, this Black skin, this human and sacred skin - it felt like black implosions. This compilation of essays reads like spiritual as well as intellectual tangents and yet I assure you, they are everything but that. For all intents and purposes in this book, I refer to "Black" as the racial classification, the verb, the noun and the adjective. The word encapsulates the complex and layered experience of skin particularly for those who "wear" that word daily, by choice and by design.

The weight is both intrinsic as well as extrinsic and this book allowed me to voice the different vantage points of how implosions feel like to me. I hope you actively engage with this book and more so, gain the liberation with which this book was born out of. I believe implosions to be the silent, inward tussles that occur within us, the subtlety depends on the choice that is made in response to them. Implosions are more like tremors that lead up to a category five earthquake. Those subtle tremors are what many psychologists and other health experts are now attributing to many mental health issues we face today, especially in the Black community. It is becoming more understood that humanity has shared responses to trauma. Trauma that has gone unnoticed, unacknowledged and/or hidden. There are a few analogies I could use to explain this phenomenon of black implosions. The one I chose to speak on in this book was provided by a colleague (Thank you Paul).

Picture abandoned buildings that collapse in on themselves. If you've ever watched a video of a building that is collapsing, the internal breakdown of the building is not always what is seen at first. Rather, the catastrophic demise of the structure is what is reported on because it is visible. That visual represents how black implosions feel like to me. The slow decaying of the sacred parts of our hearts and the systematic tearing down of our minds until one day, the implosions become an outer explosion. One big moment that was years in the making that we've worn in and as our skin becomes too loud to muffle or hide. What remains unspoken grows tentacles that then create their own personality and create a different type of skin. They create a metaphorical black bunker as it were, a type of armor we wear that is not always impervious to attacks. But one that becomes an illusion of safety and protection, some may call this a mask.

The intricacies of these implosions are housed in many parts of our being, both the seen and unseen. Many people have now woken up to this, doing as much as they can to educate us on the relationship between our bodies and the trauma lodged in them. Why is this conversation different in this book?

Well, I am a continental African woman and a transplanted Black person in America writing about it. I am a "stateless being" who had the privilege and joy of being Black in and outside of the American context. My perspective offers us another chance to see black joy and black pain from another vantage point. I am one of many Black women creating space for different ways to talk about black joy, black pain - black everything from different perspectives. Consequently, this also means adding more Black voices with myriad views on healing as well. When Black people say, "we are not a monolith", I believe, among many other things, we are stating that the vastness of ancestral joy and ancestral trauma offers many vantage points to speak and exist from. In order to truly understand black implosions, that vastness cannot be contained, denied or dismissed.

Blackness is vast, it is deep, and it is varied in its expression, Afro people know that to be true because we live it every day. The stories we all carry about our ancestral history aren't properly archived, if at all, within our history as humans. But our Black bodies are the museums, each "artifact" (the Black body) holding its own story, at times screaming at you about what the trauma is and what the joy is. As much as I may not know about the entire tapestry of Afro descendancy, I do know my ancestors left an alchemical soul print behind for me to follow. I hear them all the time: when I pray, when I observe a group of Black people dancing and having fun, when I receive that well-known black nod from a stranger as we pass each other on the street, when I hear the sound of a drum and joyful ululations. My personal favorite, when I receive a compliment from a fellow Black woman.

The Afro descendant ancestors' stories as survivors, victors, antagonists and protagonists are etched in how I choose to hear them and learn from them. Their pain and their joy are something I actively choose to engage with, and I make the choice not dwell in the past. There is a stark difference between dwelling in it and embracing it - I choose the latter, and I do so with grace and grit. By embracing them, I gain clarity and an entry point into some of my own implosions. A few things were unmasked as I did more of this healing work.

The concept of masks has been talked about spiritually and academically in different ways. But there is one man whose work was imperative to how I learned and saw the concept of masks as I was embracing the past. Inevitably, his work allowed me to see myself clearly. The man I speak of is Frantz Fanon, a renowned psychotherapist and Pan Africanist. He was one of the few psychotherapists to use psychoanalysis with Blackness in mind. In his prolific book, *"Black Skin, White Masks"* Fanon delved into so many ways to explore what he called the false sense of Self.

He believed Black people carried a false sense of Self that was created by colonization and that through decolonizing the mind, Black people would recognize these masks, heal themselves and ultimately rebuild communities/nations. As a continental African, hearing and seeing myself through this man's work changed me. I found out about him in graduate school, which angered me a lot because I felt like I should have known of him way sooner. Fanon was able to explore and reveal what the consequences of masks are.

No matter what it is we are hiding, the temporary relief is costly in ways we seldom consciously consider or understand. The more I explored my implosions, the truer this became. I believe these implosions led me to a character defining moment, where I had to make the choice to stop straddling many worlds and see the masks for what they were. Unmasking 'whiteness' then, according to Fanon, is imperative to any kind of true healing. It must start first with the individual then it moves to the collective group, but doing so requires courage. I didn't know just how courageous I was until I looked at my beautifully black implosions.

I also learned that the more I addressed them, the less hypocritical I became. It was hard initially to accept this but the necessity of taking this step became unavoidable. Who wants to believe that one is a hypocrite? But through radical acceptance, I started to see where the dissonance was because my focus had changed. I was taking things less personally especially in the moments of accepting hard truths. Addressing implosions allowed me to see how I am evolving as an entity among other entities, which encouraged me to continue uncovering my often-ignored relationship with hypocrisy.

It became very clear that hypocrisy is gluttonous because there is no end to how it continually asks a person to abandon themselves. I was being called to the next level stage of responsibility and accountability. When I chose to walk the healing walk, my willingness to evolve became larger than my fear of freedom. I wanted my liberation more than I wanted to be right or liked, and more than the fear of being wrong or disliked.

So, here I am my friend, doing what I was compelled to do by writing these essays that have manifested into a book. These essays are my black implosions, a voice, a vantage point into the vastness that is my Blackness. I wanted to find a way to express them as succinctly as possible. There were times in my life I didn't always get a chance to experience and express the full palette of an emotion or a thought. Most times, people met me at the tail end of it. What seemed to them as ramblings, or self-imposed stifles, "sassiness" or an "angry Black woman" acting out, was only part of the story. I hope this collection of essays adds to the tapestry of the gorgeous Black voices that are choosing to gently reveal and fiercely advocate for black implosions.

Let us introduce and re-introduce ourselves, at our own pace and in our own ways. That being said, here are the sounds of my implosions.

1.

What do they call me? - "Masivanda"

My father's people or tribe have the Lion as their totem/tribal animal, which is called *mutupo*. It means the attributes associated with the Lion (good or bad - mostly good lol) represent that group of people. This is the simple explanation of course, because it is much deeper than that. One of my favorite parts about having a totem is that each tribe has a chant (known as a *detembo*) that educates, celebrates and archives the totems' lineage and the ways of its people. I must also mention that a child bears the totem from their father's tribe only, as totems are patrilineal in my culture.

In my tribe, I am considered a Lioness! I am called "Masivanda" or "VaChivi". I grew up gravitating towards the first title more actually as that name literally means 'Lioness'.

As a child, I heard my father do the (shorter version) of our *detembo,* and some of my fondest memories have everything to do with these chants. As a grown woman (and as a young girl), I harken(ed) to this totem for its values which include being self-driven, perseverance, pride (both the trait and the communal identity), among many others. These values were exemplified by the different family members that I got a chance to interact with. It means that I also grew up watching multiple versions of these values being personified, for better or for worse, by fellow tribe members.

In this essay, I want to focus on the one aspect of my totem that left a deep impression on me as a child. The *detembo*. What happens when one is showered with chants (cantations and/or words) and stories of being a Lioness, a 'Masivanda'? Well, let's talk about it. The *detembo* is meant to conjure up within each person feelings of pride, honor, dignity, joy, etc. The chants are meant to remain as one of the connective tissues between the living and the dead. They can even inject humor too and lightly poke fun at some of its peoples' shortcomings.

They can be narrated or performed at traditional ceremonies, as personal prayers/meditations, at family events, in cases of emergencies, or on a random Tuesday around the house (well at least in my family home). They are also very sacred and are to be treated as such. The chants belong exclusively to each respective tribe and for some, can only be seen and spoken only by that particular tribe. In my personal experience, my totem reminded me of what I call my 'unbowed spirit', the part of me that is unconquerable. I believe this unbowed spirit resides in the place that these chants call to. Mama Maya Angelou calls it the "Pristine place", I love that.

As a child, I didn't fully understand the words in the chants because the language used is very deep. However, I did understand how they made me feel. The essence of those words wrapped around my heart like the warmest hug and the best pep talk one could ever ask for. I felt the heartbeat in these chants. One of the biggest blessings they gave me was to be in a continual conversation with the virtue of Pride. I knew who I was as a Lioness, even as a child and most often than not, I moved as such. I didn't realize it then, but pride in myself and my family, my culture and my spiritual identity as a girl-lion, served as my guiding light.

Christianity states that pride is one of the seven deadly sins, and I believe that is one side of it. Pride, as it is understood through my totem though, is not an egoic expression of power because it is not meant to be about you - only. As a matter of fact, it is meant to remind you that you are part of a group, and it is from this understanding that you build a strong sense of Self. A self-identity steeped in a fierce kind of love that fortifies you and even precedes you, and in turn forms a force field around you. One of the most intrusive culture shocks I experienced when I moved to America was the systematic tearing down of a Black person's sense of Self. It isn't always the loudest stripping of one's dignity that has the lasting effect, but the slow burn. The slow burn sullies and hides in insidious ways within the things society calls you and names you.

It usually requires you to dig deep and find identity-affirming knowledge so you can protect yourself and survive. It is my belief that this identity affirming knowledge is meant to align us to the spiritual principle of Pride. That is the privilege I have as a continental African and I have expressed this in several ways throughout this book. I have sometimes struggled with all the implosions that come from wearing this Black skin in the American context. By contrast, this Lion totem I have adorned since birth was constantly reviving me because I was wearing its skin. Poetic Justice, right?

The Pride I have in myself is something I had access to daily as a child and when it was questioned, I was usually surrounded by a plethora of knowledge i.e., the chants to legitimize my presence and essence as an African, a Zimbabwean, a Black person, a Black woman and a Lioness. No matter what I was called (especially that which was unwarranted and unwanted), I had that to stand on. And yet, in the US, it felt like I was living in a state of perpetual self-defense, feeling like I must explain or defend my afro essence. Honestly, that level of psychological and spiritual violence is not only dehumanizing, it is cumbersome and disrespectful.

The Lioness possesses graceful grit, an ethos I have worn to both survive and thrive. When I pray, I hear the ancestral whispers and roars that at times sound like an announcement, like a proclamation followed up with all the bells and whistles of a dramatic re-entrance into life's ballroom so to speak. Here she is, THE Lioness - it tickles me. I feel both unbowed and enveloped by what the ancestors decided to call me. Being unbowed is synonymous with pride, that is what I know. Even as I was writing the majority of these essays, I could feel the pride in me rise up, as the unbowed spirit danced with joy. I automatically stood up straight, held my head high and adjusted my crown.

So, what do they call me? They call me "Masivanda" - the Lioness; the one imbued with graceful grit. My healing journey has allowed me to embody and emanate this graceful grit. It is an amalgamation of the balance I have worked diligently to cultivate within me. The ancestral cauldron demands that we express and embody self-sovereignty in different ways, the tools are in that cauldron. Graceful grit is one such tool.

It is about seeing the opportunity we have been granted as Afro humans in this lifetime, to call upon all parts of ourselves so we can thrive. The Pride I have because of my totem allows me to know I can reach out to all my ancestors and move through life with grace and grit. I do not have to know it all because there is an alchemical blueprint I can follow with each step. Admittedly, it still is a little hard for me to remember this during challenging moments, but I am better at centering myself now, that's for sure.

My pride in Self is the access point to this knowledge that is readily available to me. I do not have to ask for permission or wait for external validation, it is my birthright! It exists on the continent, and it is anywhere a Black person exists. Pride allows me to recognize myself as the graceful gritty woman that I am. Pride is about identity-affirmation which is ultimately self-affirmation (my inherent dignity and worth) so I can proudly say to myself, "I am who I always thought and knew myself to be", and that belief both empowers me as much as it pleases me.

Lioness is the name that I choose to answer to.

2.

Unzip my Skin

One of the best feelings in the world is coming home from work and taking off that piece of clothing that was choking the life out of me all day, be it a bra, spanks, shoes, etc. I am presuming you know the feeling of coming home, pouring that glass of wine, a cup of tea/coffee, and lamenting about the suffocating role you had to play at work, at school or life in general. Not to mention those character traits we tap into to survive the day. I've had fantasies of being able to unzip my skin the same way I can take off my jacket.

To unzip both the inside and outside of this "Black skin" and just 'quit' being it. This skin I'm in doesn't unfurl itself in the ways other skins do in this country. Due to the bicultural vantage point I carry, I often ask myself, "How am I wearing this skin? How do I experience this 'Black skin'?". I may not have a definitive answer, but I can share my personal experience. It is a pseudo-dichotomous experience, let me explain. I have shared my favorite memory of my father doing the chants in the previous essay. Even though I may not have understood the archaic language in those chants, I remember feeling celebrated, uplifted, and rooted in a truth beyond me. I was tenderly enveloped in a kind of love that is pure and transcendent, the truth of that was hard to miss even for a pre-teen. This experience was alchemical; it was beyond skin even though my skin housed this magic.

And then there is the other side, the American experience of this "Black skin." I remember the first time I was called 'nigger,' and I didn't know how to respond. I had just started my journey in America, and in retrospect, I can see clearly how this person was trying to hurt me or provoke a response out of me. It didn't land the way he intended it. The word bounced off my skin, even though the insult was directed at my skin. This attack was meant to keep me grounded in the synthesized version of "skin"; Black skin as defined and/or re-imagined by whiteness. It was meant to hit deep and attack my core sense of Self as an Afro-descendant, but that is not how I experienced it. I bore witness, for the first of many other times to come, to the systematic tearing down of a Black body, a Black mind and a Black Soul. For those who believe racism is in the minds of Black people in the US, I can assure you that I did not go out of my way to find racism as an immigrant. Nope, it found me—an unwilling target.

Racism isn't the boogeyman, and it does not live inside the minds of Black people in the US. The terror they experience is real. Herein lies the pseudo-dichotomous experience I mentioned earlier. Even though I wear this "Black skin," the racial slur bounced off me. This was mainly because I did not see myself as the imagined Black person he was addressing with that slur. In my eyes and the eyes of my ancestors, I am a Lioness. That is the name I answer to. The skin I wear as a Lioness is steeped in Pride, Respect, Dignity, etc., and so I do not have a duplicitous view of my existence.

By that I mean that I am not in denial of who I am nor do I live everyday deceiving myself about my existence, that is what whiteness does. I could see it in his eyes that he believed I was the caricature of blackness he was calling me. On the other hand, I looked at him with bewilderment at the passion he was showing as he called me by a name riddled with hate and fear. A hate-filled manufactured name that was not mine to wear or to answer to. It was the intent and the energy behind it that I was rebuking. The surprise on his face when I did not answer or respond to it amused me a little. Because 'nigger' as he said it, is not my name nor is it my core identity.

There was a period in my childhood when I didn't get reminded that I was "black" every day, all the time. I knew I was African. I knew I was a Zimbabwean AND I knew that I had melanated skin, but I had not been bombarded with discriminatory dogma regarding blackness frequently. After a few years of living in America, I used to joke with my friends that I was the "new Black." I was half-heartedly being facetious, of course, because in some ways, that did actually ring true to me. "Transplanted Black person" or the "new Black" means I had lived in the US long enough to be considered "Black," but I still wasn't Black enough.

Since America is obsessed with labeling things, I went with "new Black". And as I mentioned in my introduction, upon returning to Zimbabwe, I had also changed "too much" to be African/Zimbabwean enough too. I had become Americanized. This created a unique space of statelessness where I teetered on the brink of potentially having my "African/Black" identity questioned on either side. That is why

I called my experience with my Black skin pseudo-dichotomous. I had to learn that in the American context, my skin (this holy and human skin) carried with it the same alchemy that I grew up knowing. Even though the power within Black skin in America was and is continually questioned, played with, as well as pacified, I was always first and foremost, a Lioness.

I embarked on a journey of self-reflection to understand what this skin I wear truly means to me. There were behaviors and expectations associated with this skin which define me as either a complete "African/Black person" or an 'outsider'. And as an "outsider," I began to notice the gaps. Initially it was painful to do so, but over time, it became a great source of inspiration and ultimately healing. It allowed me to ask questions about both of my identities as an African/Black person and as an outsider (the new Black) with joyful objectivity. This is where I explored something I call "fragmented epithets". I will discuss them further in the next essay.

By imagining myself unzipping my skin metaphorically, I allowed myself to explore healing in ways that tethered me to the Creator and to my ancestors. It became less about the imagined conceptualizations of skin color or the sometimes rigid parameters created by nationalistic identity and more about self-sovereignty. I realized that my healing journey would require me to undergo this process <u>repeatedly</u> – to unzip my skin and confront the questions I was afraid to ask but needed to. I must admit that I was apprehensive about releasing this essay, as expressing my desire to "unzip my skin" felt vulnerable and possibly like self-betrayal and betrayal of my fellow Afro descendants. It seemed like a path that could leave me exposed or could be used against me. It's a dose of what some might call "Black paranoia." I suppose.

But unzipping my skin released me and I became beholden to myself in newer ways, so I decided to share this implosion. What I came to understand is that whiteness often promotes a narrative that suggests Afro descendants have never experienced true sovereignty, both individually and collectively. We remain imprisoned to the confines of the imagined synthetic 'black skin'. Even narratives that acknowledge some form of Black sovereignty in the past often still portray us as savages in need of guidance from White people and/or the ideology of whiteness. In response, blackness becomes a space where we continually strive to prove our worth as Afro descendants, believing that 'hard work' will make us equal to this perceived "standard" of power and greatness. I also learned that I wear this Black skin not as a point of negotiation with race mongers or race deniers. My existence precedes any of these racial beliefs and so blackness as a concept in turn asks me to deny myself at times, which I cannot and will not do. When I unzipped my skin, I allowed for other truths to prevail, truths that existed before whiteness became the prevailing dogma. Truths like my tribal chant, like the Lioness skin I adorn and the ancestral calls I answer to.

Healing in this case is revolutionary because it's ancestral and not bound by political, cultural or religious dogma; it represents self-determinism and self-sovereignty. Healing transcends the 'gaze' that Mama Toni Morrison referred to in all of her books. The White, male, female, tribalistic, cultural, etc., gaze. It eliminates the need to prove oneself to others. It becomes a matter of dignity and inherent worth. It becomes less about what they call me, you or us and more about why and how I, you or we wear this sacred Black skin. It is no secret; we exist in a world filled with paradoxical forms of Power.

Healing has the potential to reintroduce us to ourselves and transform the seemingly dichotomous experience of skin, especially Black skin, into a space where healing allows our true natures to unabashedly bloom. This requires courage, the courage to metaphorically unzip our skin and be both observers as well as stewards of what we find. Hopefully, it leads us to heal, create and lead from our truest sense of Self.

3.

Being each other's missing piece and peace

Remember the infuriating moment I had earlier about discovering Pan Africanism later in my life? This essay will explain why I felt angry about it. I didn't see it coming, that's why. The spiritual awakening that most people speak of, sometimes it sounds like it is supposed to happen in a certain place at a certain moment or something. Well, my "or something" occurred during grad school. I was working through a lot of research material when I found myself steeped in Pan African theology. This powerful movement was started as a way to bridge a gap, or mend fences I guess, it depends on who you ask. The main objective was to create a theology, an ideology, and a postcolonial theoretical framework that would empower and provide a landscape to explore and empower afro identity from.

I remember the first time I read Frantz Fanon, Wole Soyinka, Aimé Césaire, Achille Mbembe and many other influential Pan-Africanists. This body of work was entirely new to me. This experience challenged me to finally accept that I wasn't as safe as I thought I was. Education had always provided me with some level of safety since I was a child. The realization that the same place that I had loved since childhood had hidden from me (in plain sight) morsels of knowledge directly linked to my freedom, broke my heart.

I was disillusioned, devastated and faced some form of despair to be honest. At the same time, I felt like I couldn't even express this pain to the staff, faculty and other fellow students at the university because I felt betrayed and ridiculous for being so "naive". What else did I expect? That an educational system that hadn't yet fully been decolonized would then provide me with decolonized information promptly? I recall wandering around campus in a daze for weeks. My emotions were a tumultuous mix of complexity and contradiction. Although I felt awakened, that feeling was accompanied by guilt, freedom with shame, and righteous anger with deep sadness.

As a continental African, one might assume that my proximity to the "motherland" would have granted me access to this knowledge. Simply being born on the continent with a natural sense of pride in my African heritage grants me self-sovereignty, right? I hung on to that illusion for a while, until my eyes were opened. Something inside me shattered when I read those wonderful Pan African love letters.

As I looked back, I realized that I had different and mismanaged expectations of the American Educational system because I had fallen for the romance of this country like everyone else had before me. The ideological romance of the U.S. was also the fuel I was running on - the fuel of Hope. The word I grew to have a contentious relationship with because I hadn't yet seen what needed to be seen. The impact of those postcolonial theorists was a paradigm shift and this African girl was reintroduced to herself once more. The strange yet familiar feeling of disillusionment allowed me to process complex feelings, and it increased my intellectual as well as spiritual landscape. I received my own brand of amazing grace.

Let me walk you through my inner black implosions with this experience. I felt guilty because I thought I was supposed to have known this information already, so maybe it was my fault that I didn't know what I should have known. I felt shame, because well, I'm African and shame is ingrained in how we process failures, even the not so clear ones. Then the sadness that masqueraded as anger followed, as I was yet again shown how erasure is institutionalized. This is one of the moments where my privilege as an 'educated' continental African burdened me because this kind of access mustn't be preserved for the few. I wanted as many Afro descendants as possible to have access to what I had just read.

More so, I hoped their hearts would break open as mine had and they would see themselves as I did then. Guilt, shame, sadness and anger were not the only emotions I felt though, they were accompanied by joy, peace, acceptance and freedom. I had become unshackled from certain half-truths and whole lies about my Blackness that had followed me all my life. The awareness I gained challenged whatever I had believed of myself as an Afro descendant, as a woman and as a human. I felt as though I had been exposed to a form of fragmentation, imposed both systematically and self-inflicted. In the moments following my exposure to this work, I had to grapple with a fragmented sense of identity. Even though I knew I was African and Black, I didn't KNOW I was African and Black. If this sounds confusing, just keep reading, hopefully that last sentence will make sense.

I mentioned before that this smart man named Frantz Fanon believed that decolonizing the mind required an awareness of a "false sense of Self." I was learning that due to our separation as people of Afro-descendancy, we had cultivated a fragmented identity around this very concept, even among the Africans who remained on the continent. We, too, were and still are blind to the truth of who and what we are as a people. I believe the solution lies in the "gap" that exists between Afro descendants worldwide. We each hold fragments of one another, like scattered puzzle pieces, like shards of glass on the ground.

A part of my healing journey involved recognizing these fragmented aspects of my identity and incorporating them into my ever-evolving Self. It also included grieving and accepting that I may not be able to recover everything needed to heal. This "rift" between continental Africans and African/Black people in the diaspora manifests in various ways including what I call "fragmented epithets." They are akin to microaggressions but within our own broad Afro community. They aren't necessarily discriminatory, but they can be prejudicial, stemming directly from our fragmented collective history.

This fragmented experience of our identity and shared history is complex. Firstly, as a Black individual, you'd have to acknowledge that fragmented epithets exist. Secondly, you'd have to see your hypocritical ways regarding them. Thirdly, you'd have to believe that as an Afro descendant, you have a role to play in healing yourself and other Afro descendants. And lastly, you'd have to be willing and to be courageous enough to participate in putting this puzzle piece of Afro joy and Afro pain back together in your own way.

I see us Afro peoples at times, as distant relatives who only possess fragments of each other's stories, filling in the gaps with our own pain and misinterpretations of what happened (or didn't happen). These interpretations manifest as anger, betrayal, shame, guilt, self-hate, frustration, abandonment, silence, confusion, and hurt. Instead of engaging in healing dialogue, we hurl fragmented epithets at each other, driven by a deep yearning for recognition and connection. A yearning for "home", a home that we strongly desire but don't know how to find. Have you ever experienced a kind of yearning so overwhelming that words fail to express it, yet the ache is so loud it demands fulfillment? The gap holds the ache but also the answers. We are each other's equilibrium, and our shared pain as well as joy serves as the ultimate equalizer and our guiding star.

I've been a nerd for as long as I can remember, loving and enjoying the process of learning so school became my safe haven, it felt like a second home. Looking back, I realize that part of my fragmented identity was solidified there. I vividly recall a primary school memory, where I was being asked this very irritating question, "Who discovered the Victoria Falls?" These breathtaking falls are one of the world's wonders and they reside in Zimbabwe (look them up). And in response to the question, all the students would eagerly raise their hands (including me) and say, David Livingston, a White British explorer sent by Queen Victoria to "discover" things in Africa and claim them for the British Empire. The dissonance began here.

In the same history class, I learned that Africans/Zimbabweans had lived there before this man "discovered" the Falls, and they had another name, Mosi-oa-Tunya, meaning "the Smoke that Thunders." But I still had to say it was this White man to pass an educational exam whose standards were set by Zimbabwe's former colonizer. Make that make sense!

I bring this up to highlight that formal education, while essential, can often be a barrier to truly healing a fragmented identity. Frantz Fanon believed in decolonizing the mind to reach one's true Self, and I concur that healing depends on accessing decolonized sources of information. The question arises: whose education are we using to connect with the "truth" that is meant to inform as well as heal us? It's clear that many educational institutions engage in erasure through their curricula, both on the continent of Africa and elsewhere. The exposure to Pan-Africanism should start much earlier than that and should be readily accessed anywhere an afro descendant resides. For those who had the good fortune to do so, you are blessed and privileged.

I attended primary and secondary school in Zimbabwe, where education was comprehensive but still limited in critical ways. Not only did I have to admit that David Livingston "discovered things" on my ancestral lands, but I wasn't informed about the experiences of my other ancestors in America and the diaspora at large. I really didn't learn about the Black people taken from African land, who endured brutality, torture, dehumanization, and death. I didn't learn how they overcame these horrors to build their own legacies earlier in my educational experience. Continental Africans can gain valuable insights from this history, which is in fact, African history. I also didn't stay informed about the state of affairs concerning Black people in the diaspora; instead, the "gap" was filled with mainstream American and European pop culture. Black Americans' apparent influence in pop culture was highlighted. And when I did hear about what was happening in the diaspora, I didn't have enough historical context. This 'educational gap' perpetuates the narrative of our separateness as Afro descendants.

My historical struggle as a continental African centered around colonialism, not slavery, yet the dissonance it created had similar overtones and undertones for most Afro peoples. The ongoing denial of who we are to ourselves and to each other further perpetuates the enduring legacy of colonization and slavery. The illusion of our separateness suggests our connection to each other ceased to exist because whiteness dictated that. This is a form of spiritual violence with real consequences for one's sense of Self, whether you're a continental African or an African in the diaspora. In Pan African theory, freedom thinking is rooted in our self-confidence as Afro peoples.

The wounds caused by the separation through slavery and colonization, as well as the feelings of abandonment and homelessness that follow often drown out the truth. <u>We are each other's missing piece, and consequently each other's peace as well</u>. Being African is not solely about your skin; it's about your essence. The motherland never truly left Afro descendants who didn't grow up there, as that implies a static identity. It came with them to the American shores and the other lands they were taken to. Believing otherwise not only leaves us vulnerable to others defining who and what we are; to them calling us whatever they wish without our consent or approval, it ultimately affects our confidence in Self, in each other and in our ancestors.

Being African is not something you lose. I believe this despite the sad comments I've heard some continental Africans make about their fellow Afro descendants, hurling different types of fragmented epithets like calling Black Americans "the lost ones." Well, let's unpack that black implosion in the next essay shall we.

4.

Deciphering the Fragmented Collective Soul

The *"Lost Ones"*

I am the daughter of a retired high school English teacher, and one of the habits I've developed over the years is looking up the definitions of words regularly. A quick Google search gave three definitions of the word I will be exploring in this essay and that word is "lost". All three definitions will apply to what I have to say. "Lost" as an adjective means:

1. *"Unable to find one's way; not knowing one's whereabouts."*
2. *"Denoting something that has been taken away or cannot be recovered."*
3. *"(a game or contest) in which a defeat has been sustained."*

The first time I heard other continental Africans speaking of fellow Afro descendants, using the above stated definitions in their tone, was when I moved to the US. I do not remember hearing this when I was in Zimbabwe, or maybe I was just too young, naive, or simply not in spaces where this was being discussed. It may be all of the above. What I do know is that the "setup" became clearer with time. The "setup" I am referring to is the pitting of continental Africans against Black Americans. It occurred in both subtle and obvious ways, whether by stereotype, by personal choice, or by design.

Fragmented epithets - that is what I call them. As I mentioned in my previous essay, fragmented epithets are akin to microaggressions in that they actually do involve groupthink and carry some effectual weight. They are notions or beliefs created by the concept of 'blackness' and live on due to the lack of information, too much information or misinformation that exists today regarding Afro peoples. Colorism is an iteration of these fragmented epithets. It is a minefield to explore but very necessary because I believe that the rift between Afro descendants has left each of us with a lopsided understanding of our collective story. The pain and misgivings in that story are marred with indelicate explanations, a bucketful of hypocrisy and a spoonful of anger with a dash of unforgiveness. This essay explores the "lost" epithet as well as a couple of more epithets. I have had to come face to face with my own fragmented epithets, both personal and inherited in order to speak with you as frankly as I could.

Due to the limited knowledge that I had about the Black experience in America, there was an immediate sense of hierarchy created upon my arrival. It took time for me to notice the patterns though, that's where the hiccups began. The "good Black person" quota is one such pattern. It is the equivalent of the "model minority" phenomenon, which is the belief that Asians are better minorities and exemplary citizens compared to other minorities, most times meaning better than Black people specifically. The "good Black person" phenomenon is typically continental Africans and/or black immigrants, who are seen as "better" because they "keep their heads down, work harder (supposedly), do not complain, show gratitude, etc."

Out of this viewpoint would be born the frustration I have heard from many continental Africans who concur with the stereotype that Black people in America are "lost and lazy." And from Black Americans, the frustration with continental Africans thinking they are "better" than Black Americans. Furthermore, the false belief that continental Africans have more access to resources than Black Americans. Before you know it, we are culprits and victims of othering each other and using fragmented epithets to legitimize our feelings, or shall I say, implosions.

"Lost" in this case is being used as a fragmented epithet to define and confine all Black Americans. Conversely, assuming all continental Africans/Black immigrants carry an air of, dare I say, 'superiority' about themselves is also another fragmented epithet. I do not subscribe to essentialism and generalizations because they breed contempt as well as lazy thinking. As complicated as our history is as Afro people, nuance is a must - always. I believe what comes off as cultural arrogance by some continental Africans who are oblivious is the lack of understanding about the Black experience in America.

Furthermore, it is that privilege I mentioned in my first essay of not growing up having my Blackness being questioned, played with and pacified daily. I have heard the phrase "lazy and lost" being used specifically and emphatically to refer to Black Americans by other continental Africans, and this was not always born out of personal experience, it was hearsay. America labeled black people a particular way and some people ran with that. And then other times, it is a miseducation of the Black experience as well as a lack of cultural awareness regarding the insidious implications of those labels. BUT it most certainly is cultural arrogance for some continental Africans - period.

However, the "setup" creates a very clear dichotomy of how "blackness" is experienced among Afro-descendants, one being seen and embodied (consciously or not) as "better" than the other. As it is with everything else, unless your eyes are opened to the suffering and lived experiences of others, to the various truths that exist outside of you, the fragmented epithets will remain siloed conversations. Until I heard and saw the ways in which "blackness" is experienced in this country, I was unaware of the 'set-up' because it can be that surreptitious. Wole Soyinka (an amazing Pan Africanist) talked about the need to look at "whiteness" as a concept and a tool for white supremacy, and therefore subsequently looking at "blackness" as a concept as well as a tool for subjugation.

"Whiteness" has a particular philosophy on power that does not allow for acknowledging and validating the emotional toll of colonization and slavery. Consequently, it does not account for the spiritual effects of colonization and slavery thereby failing to be wholly accountable and responsible. This dismissal of the soul of Afro descendants is at the core of why we are stuck, why Black Americans can be called "the lost ones" by other Afro descendants, and yet we are two sides of the same coin. A case can be made that Africa itself is lost in more ways than one. The fragmented aspects of Afro descendants do not solely begin with the geographical consequences of colonization and slavery. Spiritual colonization and slavery lie at the heart of the fragmented identities experienced by people of Afro descent. Our spiritual identity as Afro people houses both the essence and ancestry, which are the mental, emotional and physical manifestations of Power.

So, let's revisit the definitions of "lost" so I can articulate my point further. As an adjective, "lost" means:

1. *"Unable to find one's way; not knowing one's whereabouts."*
2. *"Denoting something that has been taken away or cannot be recovered."*
3. *"(a game or contest) in which a defeat has been sustained."*

I firmly reject the notion that being African or an Afro descendant is something one can "lose." The ideology of whiteness (through erasure) perpetuates this false idea of "loss" to maintain its dominance and keep Afro peoples trapped in a perpetual state of searching and self-doubt. I believe that being African or an Afro descendant cannot be taken away from anyone; it is an illusion to think otherwise. Moreover, I believe that it can be "accessed" from anywhere. This is why healing, despite its increasing mainstream appeal and dilution, remains crucial for Afro descendants to partake in.

Healing is akin to physical therapy; it's a process of reawakening an atrophied muscle. What I'm boldly asserting with this analogy is that there has never been a moment when we (Afro descendants) were not impressive, intelligent, capable, or any other powerful attribute you can think of. And yes, I am including all the ways in which we have shown up as both protagonists and antagonists in human history. African essence cannot be stripped away. As many Pan-Africanist leaders have proclaimed, no one can truly conquer, colonize or enslave you, not completely anyway- they can try, and they have tried and continue to do so. But the unbowed spirit within us will not allow it and it is an individual task to pay attention.

As for the third definition of "lost", I believe at times living in this black skin as perceived by whiteness in America, can feel like and has manifested itself like a game where white supremacy taunts us with the illusion of a level playing field. Even though the foundation of whiteness rests on the belief that only White individuals deserve to participate and win the game. A whopper of a mind game that was instituted through colonization and slavery. The pillaged 'real estate' that inflicts irrevocable and lasting damage are the remnants of a once colonized as well as enslaved Black body and mind.

This is an undeniable truth that many of our ancestors have tried to help us traverse. The collective as well as the individual minds and souls of Afro descendants remain the battlegrounds. These wounds require not just a band-aid but genuine and deliberate attention through healing. As long as we neglect or downplay the necessity of healing, Afro descendants will continue to be in a perpetual state of search and of self-doubt. Worse still, we will continue to undermine ourselves and each other. Until we heal these fragmented parts of ourselves, we will remain stuck, experiencing "blackness" as it was originally intended to be experienced by white supremacists. As stagnant energy, otherness, inferiority complexes, imposter syndrome, low confidence, a sense of loss and being lost, an abyss of nothingness - being ultimately detached from our true Self. The term "lost" in this case is synonymous with the original intent of the scientifically racist coined term, which is "blackness".

We will continue to linger on the fringes, perceiving Power as an external force, like "body things," as Achille Mbembe (another prolific Pan Africanist) describes it. We will perpetually be pacified by a narrative that portrays us as "kings and queens" without truly embodying the traits that come with the titles and without truly living as such, both inwardly and outwardly. When we are not firmly rooted in the power of our authentic ancestral identity, which includes our spiritual identity, we will find ourselves "twice defeated before we even begin," in the words of Marcus Garvey. In that case, true loss and being lost would indeed be our Afro reality.

"The Motherland"

I've wrestled with this fragmented epithet for a while, especially after my extended stay in the US. There was a romantic and nostalgic tone in the way some Black Americans spoke of Africa, seemingly detached from the realities of the continent. This sentiment often lacked a long-term vision, such as investing in Africa as Afro descendants or acknowledging both its beauty and the disparities. The truth is, you can't separate one from the other, they are intertwined. The 'gap/rift' that I have mentioned a few times kept coming to mind. It became clear that Black Americans were not taught about Africa comprehensively, much like how I grew up without knowledge of their American history. Most educational institutions, except HBCUs, overlooked African history as did Zimbabwean institutions (at least as far as I know).

I was fortunate to have geographical proximity to Africa, being born and raised in Zimbabwe. I can trace my ancestry back several generations. However, I also realized that as I read about Zimbabwe's history and then African history, I have learned that "my people" are a combination of individuals who migrated from West Africa down South during our own version of the Great Migration. This raised questions about my own identity and what 'home' means when my ancestors moved generationally. I am still looking into this by the way, and it is fascinating. How can this exploration benefit us as Afro descendants in how we discuss the motherland and each other? I believe this is worth exploring, don't you think?

It certainly reshapes our conversation about the concept of 'home.' The understanding of the motherland becomes a fluid experience rather than a rigid one. For some continental Africans, this might challenge their pride in their regional identity, inducing the need to become gatekeepers against other Afro descendants. Whilst for the Afro descendants in the diaspora, it offers an open pathway to home without fear of judgment for not knowing their origins and investigating any mismanaged expectations as well as judgments about the motherland. It's a loving, graceful and redemptive approach. Redemption for whom, you may ask. Well, redemption for all of us.

I understand the inclination to claim our Blackness and African-ness, especially for the descendants of slaves or for those who are displaced and denied access to their own land due to war, famine or any other natural or man-made disaster. However, both continental and diaspora Africans could benefit from recognizing that this 'push and pull' dynamic creates an opportunity for exploration. It's a space filled with white audacity and black rage, white fear and black joy. If we dare to explore the masks and medicine within that space, we can uncover empowering truths so we can continue the work of decolonizing our minds. The legacy of Pan African theorists is to keep exploring 'blackness' as a concept, an artifact, or a tool—an identity we can choose and use for personal growth. It shouldn't be a constant negotiation of self-sovereignty but a place to define true power. It's an avenue to get closer to our core identity as Afro descendants, independent of what we may call "home" - so we can pass onto future generations an inheritance of a home built and fortified by an unbowed sense of Self.

"A real Sista"

Here is another pain point I observed, one of many fragmented epithets that is a hindrance to our bond as sisters for Black women. Let me set the scene: a couple of years into my arrival in the US, I met an American Black man. At this point, I was accustomed to continental African men but not Black American men. The young Black man I am referring to asked me out on a date and in the process of asking me he said, "you're a real Sista". Mind you, I didn't even know there were categories of realness for Afro descendant women. And then I asked him, "A real Sista? As opposed to what kind of a Sista?". He told me that I was a "real Sista" because I was from "the continent, the motherland."

I absolutely was baffled by the "compliment" because I felt how deeply divisive it was in its myriad implications. Whether he meant to do it or not, he pitted me against other black women and also legitimized the narrative of blackness as a space for continual searching, in this case searching to be "real". "Realness" being legitimized by geographic proximity to the motherland continues to create a hierarchy of Black excellence. A hierarchy which purports that the closer you are to the continent, the more African legitimacy one possesses, and the more exceptional one apparently is right? I don't think this is true.

This encounter and a few more that followed (sad to say), would be another seed planted that would later germinate as I investigated this concept of "blackness and realness". The necessity of looking at it the way Wole Soyinka did, to see blackness as a concept and not necessarily as one's entire identity, continued to haunt me. It became a curious thought for me to investigate this damaging perception of a tier system to quality in Afro-descendant women based on their geographical proximity to Africa.

The result: well, from the many conversations I have had with Black women in the US, they believe some continental African women think they are better than them. This of course is not just in regard to men and relationships; it is one of many reasons. Unfortunately, there are some continental African women who do think they are better than Black women in the US. Cultural arrogance is a form of spiritual violence we need to talk about because some continental Africans are complicit in their silence on this particular matter as well. Some believe they are not beholden to the lived experience and trauma of fellow Black women especially because of geographical proximity. The sentiment is also felt by continental African women who feel Black American women harken to stereotypes when addressing them as well. I hope my message is clearer with each epithet I talk about.

The notion of a "real Sista" continues to push Black women in the diaspora to the fringes. And it also downplays the misogynistic ways African womanhood unfurls itself sometimes (just look at the rates of femicide in Africa). Domestic Violence/Gender Based Violence is an issue prevalent in the motherland. I am not interested in glamorized servitude masquerading as tradition. I am not interested in lip service or fake praising the majesty of the "African Queen". There is a clear distinction between the celebration of the Black woman and pacifying her - both continental African women and Black American women are staring down the same barrel of this misogynistic gun. We all know this all too well, being put on a pedestal that continually changes its meaning and its standards without our consent, approval or receiving any lasting recognition.

The "angry black woman"

This fragmented epithet is mainly used to describe Black American women negatively, most, if not all of the time. I have heard some judgments from fellow continental Africans who believe their womanhood, and how they sit in it, is "better" than American Black womanhood. Black women are too loud, too expressive, and too rambunctious they say. But this epithet is a trap because for all Black women, there is no safety in silence or speaking up in many contexts. Again, please look at the statistics of femicide in America and on the African continent, it doesn't matter if you're a woman who was taught to be obedient and silent or if you're a woman that talks back. Misogynoir comes for us all.

There is an array of crazy when it comes to Afro descendant women and their responses to disrespect. Oh yes, let's be clear, the tendency to stifle Black women's experience of emotions is hazardous to everyone's health. Especially the full palette of a thought or an emotion like anger that has taught women to find different (often implosive) ways to express this emotion. Continental African women are not incapable of being angry, they can do so loudly, quietly, and emphatically (just go to some prisons and find out how they got there). It just depends on which part of the continent you are from, because in some parts, you can actually die at the hands of men for expressing and showing anger. Or for daring to think and express yourself at all.

I have a few sisters, by blood and by choice, whose realness had everything to do with our differences as Black women. Our differing lived joys and pain alike, connected us and helped reveal how pain and joy manifest themselves within our different Black contexts. We clearly have lived very different lives as Afro descendant women across the world. In listening to each other we cannot assume each other's pain or expression of Power is more important than the other because our pain or power is unique to our respective contexts. I purport that it is NOT our way as Afro descendant women to create hierarchies. Our "being-ness" as individuals AND as a sisterhood, cannot be mandated by outside forces any longer. That too, is not our way.

I titled this essay "Deciphering the fragmented collective Soul" because the mystery that is our fragmented Blackness requires some studying and investigation. Some may think the following notion to be a "romantic" one and yet it is a truth we would benefit from hearing a lot more of. The notion is as follows: <u>we are each other's missing piece and peace</u>. Afro descendants across the world have a shared history and even if the history books (the banned ones, the lopsided-in-their truth-telling ones or worse, the ones never written) say otherwise. These fragmented epithets I write about and ones I don't, are an entry point to a larger truth.

WE are each other's missing puzzle pieces to the fragmented collective Soul. And the peace within our own secret or spoken implosions is a roadmap to sovereignty. We may not have the answers to everything but as someone who has experienced peace from what I learned from other Black women's walk; it works. I truly believe that for those who choose to follow this path, it is our way back home to our truest, peaceful selves and ultimately to one another.

5.

The wound that awakened Joy

Do you recall me saying that a case can be made that Africa itself is "lost" in the previous essay? Well, here is how that was made manifest in my life. My early view of the world was shaped by the Catholic Jesus and some hypocrisy. In this essay, I will mainly focus on the hypocrisy part. That hypocrisy created dissonance within me as a child, especially as I grew to behold the title Lioness. What I had observed was that hypocrites pushed for being right rather than promoting self-worth. This encouraged hiding behind upholding culture and tradition even if they condoned all kinds of evil to exist.

Hubris begets egoic forms of power. Power that would rather dismiss and deny than accept and atone. One such egoic expression of power in Zimbabwe showed me that men didn't believe in women's inherent worth. Not equality per se, but worth, and society would be better served if we could accept and act from that delineation. It seemed to me that men believed women were (and still are) there to serve them, both Christianity and Zimbabwean culture are aligned on this matter. The realities of life as a female in Zimbabwe were dictated by this invisible yet potent contract, one that required loyalty upfront from women to men without any guarantees of a return on investment.

It wasn't always this way though and it most certainly isn't that way now. Well, wait- I cannot say that for a fact because there are so many tribes or clans in Zimbabwe that have their own norms and traditions they value and follow. Traditions that promote 'equal trade' in which men would provide and protect whilst women nurture and nurse. I do not pretend to know if it's understood as a 50/50 thing or a 100/100 thing or a 30/70 thing, it depends on the tribe. I do not know all of their tribal ways so it is wise for me to say this now because I cannot and am not speaking for all Zimbabwean women, past or present.

What I am doing is giving you my analysis and hopefully other fellow Zimbabwean women who share the same experience will back me up. So back to what I was saying. There is an invisible contract that I observed that reminded females to be grateful, to be quiet and to follow the man. The civil and political personalities of a woman took the backseat as the cultural personalities, with all the self-serving indignation (from men) that comes with it, prevailed over a woman's worth. I couldn't trust a society that needed women during the liberation struggle to gain independence from British rule, and as soon as that independence was gained, immediately denounced women's self-agency. Society dismissed as well as denied their Power, and instead switched to curtailing it by asking those same women to "remember their place" in society. WTF!?

That quick turnaround to delegitimize women as powerful change agents threatened to erase that evidence of said agency. Evidence that would teach me as a young girl, what I was capable of. Women's roles in the long fight against British rule ranged from soldiers, spies, mothers, caregivers, military strategists, and spiritual leaders. This call for women to "remember their place" frightened and angered me when I was studying my history. Because even though I was born after the Liberation struggle, being called a "born free", the sentiment lived on in cultural tradition and it was definitely not calling for my freedom. This mandate had ordered women to be "subservient" to Zimbabwean culture and demanded that women mustn't be "influenced by Western dogma."

When I did my Master's degree, my research dissertation was based on Domestic Violence in Zimbabwe. The correlation between this historical stance and the high rates of Domestic Violence was apparent in the most devastating ways. It became clearer to me that both nationalism and traditional culture can possess self-serving norms; they can morph and mimic the narrative that prevails at that moment. They changed to meet Western patriarchal needs, African patriarchal needs, Colonization/Neo-colonization, a Global economic machine, Christian religious theology, etc. Women's worth be damned.

Therefore, in my mind, masculine power and men in general became the boogeyman... and I mean that. I taught myself not to expect anything from men, and since I had to live on the same planet with them, I had to keep them close enough to "observe their ways" but far enough to not be infected by their concept of Power. There was always something curious about men, something I liked, something I thought I wanted, and of course, something that horrified me. I couldn't figure it out until I started to put the pieces together. Here are some examples:

- When I used to play house with some of my friends as a kid, I wanted to play the husband all the time.
- I had a tomboy phase, and this was not because I did not like being a girl; I liked all the "amenities" that came with boyhood i.e., the comfortable clothes (I used to wear my brothers' clothes), the freedom to roam around, being able to make mistakes, having an actual opinion, etc.
- The first time I was home late, my dad was angry because he didn't want me to end up pregnant, and when my brothers were late, he got upset because they broke a rule.
- I raised my hand in class once, right? To contest a point made by a fellow classmate, the classmate told me that I talked too much for a girl.

I could go on and on with more examples, but at the end of the day, the point I am making is I knew as a young girl that boys/men had access to express and enjoy Power in ways that I didn't. It was ingrained in the fabric of society, similar to the insidious ways racism is. And I wanted that power because it looked like freedom. I am talking about what happens when Power is defined by only one group, and all other expressions as well as experiences of it are stifled and surveilled. I soon understood that this "free" expression of Power that men worshiped was marred with lazy thinking on their part. And the consequences of questioning it were not only deadly for women, but they were infantilizing some men.

These consequences only served to create a bigger gap between me and men, between me and other women, between me and myself; it was a gap filled with all kinds of paradoxical experiences of Power: fear/faith, poor/rich, confusion/conviction, cultural identity/individual identity, shame/authenticity, and rejection/one-ness. This fragmented epithet of a "knowing her place", of a woman's worth being questioned and surveilled allowed me to reacquaint myself with the kind of power I already had and didn't know I could experience out loud.

I clearly did not want to be a male back then (I still don't want to be, in case you were wondering), and neither did I want to live in a world where men did not exist. I believe that our individual expressions of Power as men and women exist to balance each other out. I believe what frightened me was that I felt myself denying the Power of my own femininity because it felt dangerous to exist as a powerful female. It felt unsafe to me because I had not yet experienced a man who lived from authentic manhood versus performative manhood. This historical and hypocritical stance of Power continually asked me to allow for what men called me (demanded of me actually) to take precedence over my own self sovereignty. A kind of sovereignty that is synonymous with inherent worth.

I am making a clear distinction between equality and worth. Equality is about my political identity as a citizen whilst worthiness is about my human identity. It would therefore be irresponsible of me to glorify African womanhood (the Lioness identity included) without also being honest about the invisible contracts embedded within it. Many victims of Domestic Violence, as I learned in my research, were educated women. Women's perceived sense of empowerment and inherent worth, even that which was acquired through education, didn't matter.

No woman is safe from abuse, because not only did our cultural identities at times thwart our political and civil identities as women, violence also demeaned the very worth women have as human beings. Intimate Partner Violence, Domestic Violence as well as Gender Based Violence remain dire issues on a global scale. This isn't just about equality; it is about women's worth and the fear that some men have regarding functioning from this inherent spiritual place. Have you heard of this brilliant educator named Paulo Freire? If you haven't, look him up. Amongst the many things he advocated for, one of the things he wrote about in his books that stuck with me was that he believed that most people are actually afraid of freedom. We think we want freedom until we look at what it takes to fight for it and ultimately share it with others. I keep talking about healing because as I was healing, it was about setting myself free. Free from how I have experienced and ultimately internalized the hypocritical definitions as well as expressions of Power. In order to be free from this, I needed to be real about what that entails.

Hypocrisy exists because being accountable and responsible, in the truest sense of the words, is heavy and laborious. Therefore, being hypocritical provides instant gratification, seems easier and also allows us to turn a blind eye to other people's freedoms. Remember that old adage, "do as I say, not as I do"? Exactly. Manhood as I had observed it, would ask womanhood to be subservient because that is what culture and Catholic Jesus said, never mind how it is wreaking havoc on women's overall health and wellbeing. Actually, never mind how it is also harming young boys and men, who are essentially choking on their own vomit. As much as it is hurting them, they would much rather endure the choking instead of being free from it, that is how fearful some men are.

The internalized hypocrisy regarding power that I mentioned created an unbalanced personal relationship building process for both men and women. Because of this historically earned distrust (on the men's part), I placed my trust in women exclusively when I was younger. As you can only imagine, that backfired. Throughout my life, I had always seen women as the only humans I could truly rely on. I put the word 'trust' in quotes now because, in hindsight, I leaned on women because, in my eyes at the time, they seemed to be the better choice to trust compared to men whom I considered selfish and malevolent. I genuinely held this belief, and it seemed justified to me. Quite honestly, the jury is still out on that.

As you can imagine, women were like the epitome of goodness, or at least that's how I chose to see them as a way to feel safe. Despite having brothers, nephews, uncles, and male friends, as well as sporadic dating experiences throughout my life, there was always a significant part of my heart that carried what I now recognize as deep-seated anger, distrust and ultimately fear toward men (and their understanding as well as expression of Power). I cannot tell you if I have ever felt truly safe around men.

What I eventually learned over time, through harsh reality checks, is that both men and women are capable of causing harm as much as they are capable of inspiring BIG love– after all, we're all human, right? But more importantly, I realized that unhealed wounds distort one's perspective, which leads to significant blind spots. What I know now is that I was allowing my unhealed parts to govern my outlook on and experience of Power - self sovereignty specifically. Firstly, building trust and safety within myself was and is my responsibility. Secondly, learning to accept that safety in the world will mostly be experienced subjectively was a necessary perspective shift. Lastly, safety has levels to it because it isn't necessarily an absolute.

    I couldn't see it at the time due to the dissonance, which is why it is imperative that any inner discord regarding imbalanced views on power be addressed (individually then collectively) as early as possible. Picture me continuing on my life journey with this imbalanced perspective and a sharp sword in my hand as the Lioness that I am. I would unknowingly continue harming potential allies and even myself. I made mistakes. My skewed understanding of human nature kept me in messy female relationships longer than I needed to be in them. It delayed the building as well as the nurturing of respectful relationships with men that I now have. It was an indication that balance in all things really does matter and with that, I willingly and courageously went on my healing quest and began the task of unmasking and nursing those wounds.

The pain I endured at the hands of other women helped me let go of the rage and pain that mirrored their own. I finally understood that all wounds can either be medicine, poison, or both. Mine were both, and like venom from a snake, they eventually healed me. This wound became a pathway to joy. A kind of joy that allowed me to look at hypocrisy with humility and curiosity. I experienced my own identity crises, coming face to face with my own inherited hypocrisies masquerading as Power. I made the choice to tap into these two things: my ancestral wisdom and the dark feminine rage- turns out that delicious combustion freed me.

I endured multiple black implosions that kept me focused on the concept of Power, specifically self-sovereignty. I imploded as I realized that the invisible contract I mentioned earlier was occurring in all kinds of relationships in my life. After years of living in both the US and Zimbabwe, the relentless tests I experienced that had all demanded that I prove my worth at every turn, finally I conceded to the fact that I was exhausted. The hypocrisy pointed me yet again to a bigger truth that I had to contend with. Was my worth something I was willing to compromise in order to be equal? Equality as an ideology has its place but at times the price to be paid feels too steep for me. As humans we can project our own flaws and illnesses onto others, pushing each other to participate in, yet again, another circus act of proving our worthiness. How does that work when we have made power and worth mutually exclusive?

As it is with many things, I have said in my essays thus far, I had to look at my implosions and dare to create a new foundational relationship with Power. Instead of retaliating or harboring anger, I shed my armor. I didn't even want to fight in the ways I was being provoked to, there was absolutely nothing to prove anymore. I heard them again, the whispers and chants of all my ancestors, as they reminded me of who I am as a powerful Lioness. These whispers beckoned me back Home to Self, asking me to reconsider what life/society/culture had pushed me to believe about myself and about power. I had to look at the ways in which I (mis)behaved in order to be free from these invisible contracts, asking me to reconsider what Power means.

Did I want to experience Power that thrives on dismissing and denying my worth and that of others, or do I want Power that radically evolves me, a Power that is willing to accept and atone as the occasion arises? Freedom requires a kind of stewardship that repels self-centeredness and lazy thinking. It requires mature and redemptive eyes that champion the truth regarding the human condition. We are paradoxical creatures: we are liars/truth-seekers, freedom-lovers/fickle, tempted/disciplined, giving/ruthless-takers. Where the immature and judgmental eye may want us to believe we have no choice but to indulge in inherited hypocrisy, freedom asks us to courageously choose the truest path anyway.

I finally comprehended the question that God and my ancestors had been asking me amidst all the hypocritical ways of existing when we believe in the version of Power that seeks to destroy or harm. Amidst all the tears regarding what felt unjust, heavy, and cruel. In the face of some really hard things God and my ancestors asked me, "What is there to prove or defend?" I had worth that preceded the unkempt vanity of men and the stifled rage of women. It was a wake-up call for me to drop my armor because it had been a distraction, a merry-go-round of Zimbabwean-ness, of Blackness, of humanness, of woman-ness - of black implosions.

The real work was in returning to the truest sense of Self, to the place where GOD resides, the Pristine Place. A place of self-sovereignty, where worthiness and power are One. No competition, no debate and no proving anything to anyone. And it is from this place that I now both love and fight.

6.

Navigating the Middle Passage:
the inner journey from "there" to "here"

The "Middle Passage" is a chapter in Afro descendant people's history that is a devastating one. It anchored my writing journey for this book. If you recall the 'weeping episode' that I mentioned in the Preface, I stated that calling on the Black ancestors on this American land changed me. The Middle Passage was a major part of the reason I wept. After that prayer session, I found myself engaging with African American History quite differently. Instead of reading the history with a sense of unspoken and unacknowledged separation or even detachment, I asked myself an illuminating question. Did the Africans on those ships ever think they were anything other than Africans?

I stopped crying as the realization sank in like it hadn't before. The humans on those ships were still Africans before they became whatever it is they would become or be called during slavery. The horrendous and dehumanizing things that occurred on those ships did not only spiritually violate the soul of afro descendants, but they laid the groundwork for one of the most hideous forms of slavery to ever exist on earth, chattel slavery. This essay explains the connective tissue between this particular historical point and my healing journey through the following two viewpoints:

Viewpoint #1:

The Middle Passage was one of the stages of the Transatlantic Slave Trade, the forced voyage that enslaved Africans endured as they were transported from African land to the Americas and everywhere else. During this period, the enslaved humans were forcefully removed from their ancestral lands, branded, chained, and forced to reside below the decks of slave ships under deplorable conditions. They would continue to be stripped of their humanity by enduring barbaric living conditions in those ships for months on end until they arrived on the American shores. One of the costs endured during this historical stage was the inhumane erasure of their voices which were drowned out, literally and figuratively. I can only imagine that this voyage was marred with rage, sorrow, terror, disbelief, dissonance, grief, confusion, and so much more.

These human beings were still Africans until this slow and steady work of brainwashing started on those ships and continued on to the American land and elsewhere. "Home" was probably still fresh in their minds, which may have both fortified as well as tortured them, but I can only speculate on this. Nonetheless, this stage was uncertain because whoever they were going to be or whatever it is they were going to be called was no longer in their hands.

Some of the "choices" they were faced with on the ships to maintain some kind of dignity and freedom haunt me, including mothers throwing their newborn babies in the water to drown so they didn't become enslaved; or some people attempting and sometimes succeeding to take their own lives so they could not be enslaved. They were still African during this horrifying stage. Both their pain and triumph echoed loudly as I thought of how these Africans were branded and rebranded, called by whatever names the system that prevailed at the time gave them and yet still they LIVED. That is a type of alchemical Power from which I drew inspiration from as I explored the minefield of African-ness and Blackness.

Viewpoint #2:

The "Middle Passage" (with all due honor and respect) has loosely become an allegorical name that I used to describe the journey I am on. I explore the spiritual bloodline that connects me to these American shores and attempt to integrate all the ways in which the term "home" has taken on many meanings for me now. "Home" is African soil, it is anywhere a Black person lives, it is this skin I wear, it is the pristine place where only GOD, (the God of my understanding) resides. Healing is about a willingness to become anew in as many ways as your eyes are open to seeing that which is wounded within you.

I was compelled to investigate the ways in which I exist as an African- 'educated' immigrant woman, on the continent and in the diaspora. The "Middle Passage," in my imagination, is the space where the umbilical cord was cut and where I, the stateless child, am now beginning to reorient my mind to. It is a place I did not and still do not fully know but that place has been violently uncomfortable. A place where I have made some hard choices and sacrifices, a place where my ancestors continue to walk with me asking me to do better. It is a place imploring me to see things clearly, to act with foresight and courage, to be more grateful for the price they paid and to live life like I know they suffered greatly on my behalf. From this place, the ancestors urged me to live a promise they could not, and did not get to experience, and to continue to believe in leaving behind a better inheritance for future Afro descendants.

I often try to imagine what the emotional experience of all the enslaved people was like in this stage of the slave trade. What did they believe about themselves as they were at the bottom of these slave ships, being hauled off to foreign lands? What did they believe about themselves when they were enslaved in their own homelands, owned by their own people? Was being colonized a "better" hand to be dealt rather than to have been enslaved everywhere else because at least you stayed 'home'? Did they even know they were still powerful Africans even though this was happening? Unzipping their skin during this stage, one can only imagine what that skin would have professed and confessed.

I am learning to grasp the following lesson about this part of my healing journey - I cannot and will not be truly free if I am unwilling to question what I have been taught thus far about who or what I am, even if I am a continental African. Our story thus far as Africans possesses complexities that deserve exploration whilst implementing radical truth-telling, compassion, and graceful grit when assessing them. Radical truth-telling is a rather hard process to engage in when some of the information that exists about us as Africans is constantly used to legitimize whiteness.

The notion that Africans were wild barbaric savages who needed White people to civilize us prevails today. Sure, human history shows us that enslavement and the most barbaric tactics included in this essay are not unique to one group. White people may not have invented slavery, but they did make some major barbaric changes to it that are unique to white supremacy. Radical truth telling is being able to see both our antagonistic and protagonistic ways with an unhypocritical lens. Or at the very least, not dismiss or deny hypocrisy where it surfaces and then conflate issues to hide from our feelings of shame as well as guilt. Erasure may make it difficult to decolonize materials that ought to assist in radical truth-telling, but we must keep our eyes on healing anyway.

What does healing and accountability look like with this in mind? Well, it took America 400-plus years to "civilize" itself using uncivilized tactics. The hypocrisy of thinking that any human being is better at "civilizing another" is moot, instead, maybe we are doomed to accept that humans are a rather nihilistic species. Maybe the sober-minded would agree that the truth about healing and accountability is somewhere in the fringes and in the in-between. Between the slavery deniers and the self-loathing Afro descendants, that "Middle Passage" has some secrets and solutions. As an "educated" African, I have lived and have been taught to believe in facts, created by a colonial educational system enforced on us as Afro descendants. I did 'discover' there are many ways to learn, to educate, to explore, to excavate as well as to heal. I hold on to this stage of our shared history as Africans, as a way to anchor myself in truth.

There are many illusions we have been sold as Afro descendants, one of the biggest ones being our separateness. The belief in a concept of "home" that continually erases our connection to each other, to alchemical Blackness by placing emphasis on how "lost" we are. There are many detrimental aspects of displacement, when one is ripped forcibly from their mother's womb. I hear that a mother never forgets their child, even though this illusion of separateness has turned that saying into a myth, it is still a heartbreaking truth we have yet to unpack and face. What gives me some semblance of solace is holding on to the belief that the bond between mother and child still exists anywhere that child is. That the bond is bigger than erasure or any misgivings between that mother and child because then that would mean our connection as Afro peoples can never truly be "lost".

I choose to believe that for every wound caused by erasure, healing steps in to soothe that wound. I choose to believe that healing isn't about bringing all that was "lost" back, but rather about honoring what is in the present as a reflection of what survived and continues to live as a roadmap. A roadmap we can choose to burn with righteous indignation or pick up and build on. Whatever it may be, I hope we choose wisely.

7.

Unmasking the complexities of Spiritual Violence

America can be such a 'vortex' I learned very quickly. A spellbinding vortex that has a tendency of entrapping those who wear this Black skin. I also learned that the concept of "blackness" wasn't always seen as something to demystify in the US. As a consequence, this perception had a few people in a chokehold, like a magic spell. This spell promotes siloed conversations around the concept of skin color, such that any outside voice is sometimes deemed hostile.

When in fact, the multiplicity of views on this topic matters as it shows the dangers of having siloed conversations over something that affects millions of Afro descendants all over the world. I say this because the most contentious experience I have had with "blackness" in America has been between Black people who are searching for "Home" and those who are overprotective of their unique experience with Blackness in the American context. The latter group (intentionally or not) sometimes ends up monopolizing Afro-DNA altogether. Does that make sense? Any "outside" input into the conversation about 'blackness' feels like a personal attack versus another valuable addition to the Black experience.

Let's be clear, I am not talking about the Afro descendants who are blatantly disrespectful towards the Black American experience. I know they exist. And I acknowledge that foolishness exists. I am talking about the kind of gatekeeping that creates unnecessary blockages (continental Africans do the same thing in their own way as well). The latter group monopolizes Afro-DNA in ways that create limitations in how we communicate with one another, therefore perpetuating the vortex. In other words, what is only known as truth in America regarding blackness, truly can and HAS hurt Afro descendants in this country. The Afro descendants who "search" for home are the ones who were fed and half-believed the lie (masquerading as a fact) that they are 'incomplete'. The search for "home" that many Afro descendants embark on at some point in their lives in this country is sullied by the false belief of them being the "lost ones", implying some kind of defectiveness.

Let me be clear again, healing can include the voyage back to Africa, which many American Black people have done and continue to do. And to those who have followed that 'yearning' (not searching) for home, I am so proud and relieved for you. I may not know what it is like to have grown up being taunted and dehumanized because of the color of my skin. I may not know what it is like to yearn for a home that was literally ripped from you. I may not know what it is like to be the family in our collective African Family tree that is constantly shunned for being "different."

But I do know what it's like to be haunted by history and the ghosts within those echoes that call to you, asking you to listen and to follow that call. I am attempting to make a clear and respectful distinction between searching and yearning. The former continually perpetuates the false belief that our existence as Afro peoples is because of whiteness. Whilst the latter emphasizes that Black people were never lost, never stopped being African and as a people, whiteness does not grant access to our spiritual inheritance, it is already ours. It is a misleading and hurtful notion that American Black people are seen as the 'strays' in the Afro descendant family tree therefore they go searching for home because they are "lost". I mentioned this before when I was talking about the "*Motherland*" fragmented epithet.

'Lost' is also the premise for the concept of blackness. The spiritual violence embedded in the search for home is directly correlated to the 'success' of chattel slavery because whiteness almost destroyed an African body's inherent worth. A worth that is based on merely existing as an African person, firstly. Secondly, worth cannot be and will never be bestowed upon Black people through an inherently flawed system of supremacy. Consequently, in order to find completeness, this group of beautiful souls must remain in a perpetual state of searching. A kind of searching that can induce stuck-ness and a frustrated belief that they are indeed incomplete and therefore are as inadequate as whiteness purported. I really hope you can hear me on this.

Spiritual violence is about the aftermath. It is like living in a constant state of dissonance because it is clear that "whiteness" chooses to keep the focus on the disadvantages of "blackness" instead of showing the many ways one can become unstuck from its limitations. It therefore makes sense to me that other lived experiences of how Black skin unfurls itself be explored and that maybe this process can help put some pieces of the puzzle together. Some may say, well the door is always open for Black people to live differently in the US (or to even leave the US), and that is true. Some afro descendants have made that choice and are deliciously happy in their homes in the US or wherever they chose to reside on earth. BUT what truly happens to those who choose to stay in America though, those who choose to heal in the birthplace they have only known as their home?

My mother once told me something that has remained with me till this day. This was during all the protests after George Floyd's murder. She stated that the "US is seeking to rest and yet there are dead bodies walking all over that land". I was shook-eth y'all. It is the tradition of our people (Afro descendant peoples) to carry out burial rituals as a form of honor and spiritual completion of the life that was lived in this physical realm. Burial rituals are not just ceremonies performed for the heck of it. They are the completion of an Afro life, of Afro identity, of Afro essence, and of Afro humanity. Hence, not only are the Black bodies that live on this American land, being buried on land that is not their ancestral home (for the most part, I realize there is literature saying otherwise), but there is no complete acknowledgment of their humanity by the ways in which they are (un) seen, (un) heard, murdered and un-buried.

What are some consequences of this then? The counter-productive ways in which this conversation is handled at times. How can we talk about spiritual violation when the idea of Afro descendant spiritualism is not even acknowledged as a real thing by 'whiteness' and other black people as well? This became one of my North Stars on how to explore the many fragmented aspects of our soul as Afro descendant peoples. As I thought more about this topic, my heart ached for the spiritual violation against the Native Americans/Indigenous peoples as well. And the ways in which they too are restless souls of this land, who did not get their own completion in their own traditional ways and on their own land at that.

Spiritual violence is an actual legitimate argument and yet whiteness immediately denies African spiritualism because it is and was 'declared' barbaric. We are steeped in denial as well as restlessness and therefore moving forward is delayed. Spiritual violence is at the heart of what perpetuates the stuck energy that surrounds racial conversations. An iteration of power that chooses to deny and dismiss is what created whiteness, not a kind of power that chooses to accept and atone. Therefore, the stuck energy interferes with healing altogether. If there is no acknowledgment, no deep sincere path created to move towards peace that includes radical truth-telling, accountability, and responsibility, stuck-ness is the reality this conversation exists in. It is important that I repeat this statement. There are individuals as well as institutions that tend to diminish, deny and dismiss the cultural as well as spiritual expression of Power by others.

The spiritual essence of Afro descendants is a real premise for identity formation, contrary to what 'whiteness' may purport. The tendency to diminish all I just said as "ghost stories", "witchcraft", "demonism", etc., when in fact that is how Power is expressed and experienced by many Afro descendants around the world is the typical and disrespectful response. We, Afro descendants, have heard these responses many times before. It is apparent in the denial and lazy thinking that constantly take hold yet again of conversations regarding race relations hence the stuck-ness ensues, no progress is made, the pacification continues, and it is business as usual. It was and will always remain about what Power is (and is not), who gets to define it, and what gets to matter. The power belongs to those who assign meaning to things and have the resources to institutionalize them. There is a fringe created, a place where Blackness remains a constant space for negotiation and pacification when in fact that is not who or what we are at our essence as Afro descendants. We are not people of the "fringe" and yet "blackness" was created and implemented with that in mind.

Marcus Garvey expressed this same frustration by relaying that confidence in who we are (as Afro descendants) is the key. Spiritual violence is related to how we feel about ourselves, our confidence which in turn affects how we execute anything. We can only get there when we embark on one of the most crucial journeys there is, which is to accept our sovereignty and make amends for the violation against our soul/spirit as Afro-descendants. Making amends is twofold here, one part is for society at large. The other part of this is our individual work as Afro descendants to heal from the direct spiritual violation against our confidence and all the ways we participate in those violations.

We do that by acknowledging the spiritual violation against the masculine and feminine powers in us as Black men and Black women. We do that by protecting each other, even the village idiots whom we must call out when they are acting up. We do that by courageously protecting our individual expressions of Blackness even if we may not always understand said individuality. We do that by investing in each other in all the big and small ways that count, including spiritually. We do that by choosing not to add to the ways we are already violated by those who do not care for our overall wellbeing. We do that by investigating as well as challenging our long-held beliefs about ourselves and giving ourselves permission to change our minds. We do that through sacred vulnerability and leaning on ancestral wisdom wherever we can find it so we can add to healing our African soul print.

What each of us does matters in the African village, no matter what capitalism, neoliberalism or any other supremacist dogma says. Healing is not only necessary; it is in fact revolutionary and our salvation as African descendants.

8.
Erasure's Echo

I read a book written by Saidiya Hartman called "*Lose Your Mother*" in college years ago, and it spoke to me in magical ways. It is a historical memoir, a journey taken by Saidiya as she traces her genealogy. She specifically targets the "forgotten slaves," the ones whose names are not recorded in history. So, she travels to Ghana, visits historical sites such as the Elmina Castle, and follows the slave trade route in Accra, a journey I wish for Afro descendants around the world to take, including myself and other continental Africans. Saidiya interacts with Ghanaians and Afro Americans who have lived in Ghana. These interactions produce this revelatory book, which is a complex amalgamation of capitalism, dominance, slavery, kinship, and ancestry. This book was a clear example of the distinction I was attempting to make in my previous essay. Saidiya's journey is what yearning looks like, and it felt like I was on the journey with her! It left me with a few questions, like "what is the success of Saidiya's yearning for 'home'?" What reprieve or solace does her journey provide for ALL Afro descendants?

My healing journey did involve my own version of yearning, and I leaned on the wisdom of the "living descendants of the forgotten slaves", like Saidiya. I remembered Saidiya's book as I started this healing journey because some of what I write within these essays echoes her findings. Her research into the "forgotten slaves" problematizes not only the romanticization of Africa as the "motherland" but also what being African means. Within her intricate and intimate analysis, she excavates the myth of home and the myth of the mother. She explores how the mother and home are both synonymous and antonymous to a child's experience of love, truth, safety, and protection. I was fascinated deeply by this juxtaposition because I believe some of the dissonance we have as Afro descendants comes from this very same place.

As I am learning about this African/Black skin I adorn, the same questions arise about what home means, what is truth, safety, love, and protection when you have Black skin? What is home and being mothered? Home in terms of geographical location; home that is our blood relations and/or kinfolk; home that is our Black skin; and the home that is our Afro (spiritual) essence. What is mothering? Mothering in all its many forms - through blood, kinship, fellowship, political governance, and relationship with the Creator. Identity formation, especially love of Self, requires some understanding of what one or all of these many things mean to each of us individually and collectively. Otherwise, we remain tethered to the masks, to the many worlds that cause an imbalance within us which almost always affects our confidence.

My implosions around this are still on-going because African soil carries with it a kind of elusiveness that frustrates me. My relationship with that soil has also contained the invisible contracts I have talked about. Contracts where truth, love, safety and protection have been violated in the name of tradition, globalization and progress. Love and truth are arguably some of the most deeply needed foundational elements to identity formation. In Saidiya's book, love and truth both have a heavy cost in the relationship between a "child and its mother." This relationship could stand in for a Black person and their definition as well as experience of "home"; Black people and Black skin; Afro descendant peoples and their connection to the Creator or GOD.

Saidiya portrays love as a quality that caused slaves a lot of pain. She states that love promoted forgetfulness (erasure) on the part of the slaves. Because of this love, ample room was created for outsiders to settle in our homes and our minds whilst the slaves' pain of losing family is somewhat eased. She also purports that love reimagines the role of the slaveholders to that of mothers and fathers. Furthermore, slave ownership and claiming kinship in her eyes, are synonymous acts to love because both of them carry the need to deprive. To deprive someone of land, property, or any possessions in the name of love. Yikes - this is deep, and she is right.

The masks we wear and the false identity that ensues are about the room we have made for outside perceptions and fragmented epithets to tell our story. Furthermore, the room we have created to have these narratives permeate our soul and introduce confusion where there need not be any. We have harmed ourselves because we have reimagined the role of capitalism, neoliberalism, etc., as our mothers and fathers. In so many ways, we have accepted that the acts of greed and self-aggrandizement we ingest daily are synonymous with power and progress, with self-love and self-sovereignty. We have allowed the love of "hustling" and reaching the proverbial mountain top to teach us to forget our truest selves. I don't think as people of Afro descent we have wholeheartedly released ourselves from this diabolical experience of love. Not just love, but also truth, safety and protection as dictated by whiteness. Hence ancestral wounds can still create disruption in our present lives because we have not engaged in the complete process of detangling ourselves from an unrequited and empty kind of love. Unrequited in the way that Saidiya expressed, that we somehow still allow ourselves to create space for whiteness whilst in its foundational principles it was created to violate our pristine places.

It is a kind of love that asks us to give and forgive without atonement, that is not love at all. That is a shitty contract! That is the invasiveness and treachery deeply embedded in invisible contracts. This kind of love continually asks us to prove ourselves, to self-surveil, to self-loath and ultimately betray ourselves. It would explain why we experience such a disproportionate amount of self-hate within the Afro community, i.e., child marriages, colorism, domestic violence and femicides, molestation, skin bleaching, inner city shootings, knife crimes, FGM, sex/child trafficking, human trafficking, etc. On both the African continent and in the diaspora, our search for home and for love seems to haunt us in ways we are either in denial of or shrug off as a problem for the "lost ones," which usually means people like Saidiya, the descendants of the "forgotten slaves."

She repeatedly echoes her idea of "home" throughout the book; in one way or another, she imagines home to be a place where she no longer feels like she is a problem, is seen as a problem and is treated like a problem. How could she not when we label the diaspora as separate from continental Africans? The "lost ones"? Yes, I am back to that fragmented epithet again. I mean really though, how can we say that in the face of some horrendous things that we do to ourselves on that continent as well? It is the highest form of hypocrisy that makes me both angry and sad for how disrespectful, petty and inherently shortsighted that epithet is.

Healing plot twist: in my own healing expedition, I am learning the ways in which I was 'lost'. Geographical proximity to Africa shielded me from some hard truths, including seeing how "home" has "forgotten" the rest of its children. Like how safety is still something I feel paranoid about when I am around other Afro descendants. Like how I haven't always been a gatekeeper of truth telling to preserve the soul of Afro essence. Like how I haven't always protected my pristine place from outsiders who only want to love me after they have reimagined my Blackness. Like how I haven't always understood how loving myself is part of my contribution to society. Like how straddling many worlds causes an imbalance with dire consequences.

    I have mentioned thus far that the issue for me was I did not know I could claim the entirety of my history as an Afro descendant. That means also acknowledging that a major part of my heart and history is scattered all over the world. Erasure has done some horrendous damage, but I urge you to call upon your own unbowed spirit, the ancestors, the spirit of the "forgotten slaves" and remain open to hear what echoes back to you.

9.

African hair/Black hair: My perspective

Let's talk about it. Similar to my experience with skin, Black hair was a topic I saw through a bicultural lens. You see, when I moved to America, I wasn't immediately aware that "Black hair" was being weaponized and demonized in American society. At Black beauty shops or "stoop salons" (i.e., getting hair done at your friends'/families' house), hair was free to exist away from the white gaze as Toni Morrison wrote, but not everywhere else. I did not know that quite yet.

Remember, I was coming from a country where my hair is 'normal', it is normal everywhere. In my immigrant eyes, I was unprepared for this culture shock because as the

Lioness that I was becoming, my hair existed in all the forms befitting a queen. And I most certainly did not have to self-surveil when I was growing up. This dissonance however, didn't last for very long like the other illusions I had experienced thus far. I can't quite tell you why, but it resembles something like the unbowed spirit I mentioned earlier.

In all honesty, I was quite shocked that 'Black hair' was even a topic when I arrived in the US, but that is the benefit of being raised on the African continent. Hair in Zimbabwe, in all its different textures and styles is such a "normal" topic and state of being. I attended college in America and one fine day, I was invited to speak in a humanities class concerning Black hair, and the central book being studied was called "The Black Girl Next Door" by Jennifer Bazsile. There is a chapter where she talks about hair and mentions all the challenges that "good hair/bad hair" had on her as she grew up.

I related in some ways to her experience but then I was soon to learn I was unqualified to speak on this topic. In retrospect, maybe I should have turned this opportunity down, but I was still new to the country at the time and had not yet learned the depths of this issue. When I presented in this class and talked about my hair, or rather I should say, the experience of "Black hair," I soon realized that I was not the "Black" that the instructor wanted. Or at least the Black that would match the tone necessary to authenticate the narrative of the book. I still have moments now where I am like maybe that wasn't such a bad thing after all. The first thing I said (my disclaimer to the class) was something to this effect. I grew up in Zimbabwe most of my teenage life, all I know of concerning hair is how tedious it felt to sit and get it done. That's it really, I didn't have much to say.

Hair care was a part of my culture, but not my entire cultural identity or cultural experience. Therefore, I could not pretend to relate to the detrimental effects this had on Black women's identity and rights as American citizens since I wasn't either of those things. I never had to worry nor had been systematically attacked because of my hair as a child and as a young adult. Whether my hair was braided, locked, plaited, weaved, or completely shaved off - I existed as I did. The fact that this was even a topic both hurt and baffled me, but hopefully my experience during that class continues to show the clear harm and absurdity of surveilling Black hair.

In some ways, that perspective needed to be heard, not as a way to drown out the voices of American Black women, but to highlight the absurdity of this matter as I mentioned. And to also hear this issue without feeling the need to pity

Black women either. I started to feel like some White people could only understand black plight through pity, which isn't necessarily a good thing. Pity presumes Black women are beggars in this conversation and maintains the need for the "White savior" mentality. Pity is a false and misleading prism to view Black womanhood through because American Black women are NOT beggars. They are American citizens using their civil and political personalities to make their stance known and to have this issue heard. An issue that shouldn't even be an issue.

However, because it was made an issue, addressing this matter is about respect, dignity and privacy quite honestly. Why the need to be intrusive about how I wear my hair? You might as well ask me what color my lingerie is because yes, that is how invasive that is. Hair was "just hair" when I was growing up, and the messages I saw and heard were more about nurturing my hair because it was just as much a part of me as any other body part. I also have to mention that this message may have been based on my nuclear/immediate family's experience and my own personal ethos as a girl-lion. I was a little rebellious about certain things including all things grooming young girls for men's attention and pleasure. But to a larger extent, when I attended school from kindergarten until the end of high school (and this also depended on if you attended a public and/or private day school or boarding school) hair was not a 'factor.' It was policy at the Catholic boarding school I attended to shave our hair off, so we had very short hairdos. The purpose of shaving it was that hair could possibly be deemed or seen as a "distraction"; you won't worry about what your hair looks like if you don't have any, right? (Sidenote: The defeminization of girls and women as well as the devaluation of feminine energy to protect boys and men from themselves was also a factor here. That's an implosion I will share another day).

Only until we were seniors in high school was there this "initiation into womanhood" as Bazsile stated. Hair felt a bit more like a ritualistic aspect of my womanhood; you were proud of it and cherished it more because you didn't have it before, so you explored and played with it- kinky and all other hairstyles in between. And I also related with Baszile regarding her own frustrations with her hair. I had to learn to love my hair, in all its distinct attributes, and love wearing it the way I wanted to. I can only speak for myself here and say that I too, like India Arie, really knew that I was not my hair. When I arrived in America and started to witness how the perception of hair could affect a person's livelihood and personhood, it was discombobulating. It still is.

What I learned years later after this experience in college and after claiming the story of my ancestors who lived on American soil, was that internalized racism didn't skip me as a continental African. As part of "hair care" or initiation into womanhood, continental African girls and women used to go to salons to have our hair relaxed, or we did it ourselves at home. We used to put chemicals on our heads, and it wasn't always based on the same historical premise as America. The premise in the US is that corporate America (and most society in general really) demands that hair standards be according to "whiteness" otherwise it actually affects your livelihood. But my eyes were opened to the remnants of colonization on our identity as continental Africans as well because there was absolutely no reason to put chemicals in our hair, and yet, we did.

Let me be clear yet again. I am not the kind of person who believes in surveilling women - period. One can wear their hair as they wish to wear it, including using chemicals. But the fact is, straightening Black hair or skin bleaching were still practices being done as part of 'beautifying' ourselves on the African continent. I am not sure that all girls and women who did these things were conscious of the underlying reasons why this would be a form of spiritual violence (and literally a health issue). And for those who were aware, their choice to do so may have been laced with self-loathing. Not everyone is willing to admit to this of course, which is why I will also say the choice to wear hair naturally doesn't always reflect self-love either. This conversation has always been deeper than that and for those who are willing to heal from their own hypocrisy regarding this matter, I am right there with you.

Healing point: In the American context, hair has intense repercussions for Black women. Multiple accounts from Black women in corporate America exist to confirm this, and Black students being banned from participating in sporting events, class activities, etc. This also happened in South Africa. The internalization of this pain in some Afro-descendant women is in rejecting the natural inherent beauty of their being-ness. This isn't just about hair. Healing ourselves is being able to see as well as accept that our hair is a part of us, and only we get to define how we feel about it, how we "wear" it, and ultimately how we embody it. (I thought the Crown Act legislation was an apt name for this because it is, in fact, a crown). But then I saw the subtle ways in which colonization left the same imprint on the minds of some continental African women. That we pursue the virtues of white femininity, including how we wear our hair, skin bleaching and yes, even how we consume cosmetics. It is almost like we're sleepwalking in some ways, like we're 'lost'. I was beside myself with grief and joy because the illusion had been shattered. The illusion that geographical proximity made me somehow immune to internalized self-hate, the bubble burst. I remain curious about these illusions and investigate them joyfully because it excites me to befriend the truth regarding them.

It took a Black American woman, a supposed "lost one", an Afro descendant of the "forgotten slaves", to remind me of our heritage as Afro peoples and to remove the blindfolds that some Africans on the continent all too often think they do not have. These illusions are many, but we do not always see them because we are so close to "home." It took being removed from my environment to see the illusions left behind by the remnants of "whiteness". And how dangerous it is to believe that we as continental Africans are somehow immune to these remnants. As I heal, I am learning that by looking at the wounds of other Afro descendants, I am compelled to automatically look at my own. I meant it when I said we are each other's missing piece and peace. My stewardship of this skin (and hair) that I adorn requires a continual assessment of my personal ethos. To see whether the ground I stand on is solid, and not bravado, not some misguided sense of African pride.

10.

It is almost always about RESPECT

Ms. Aretha Franklin had to write a whole song about RESPECT because this concept is one of the most crucial things in all human interactions. I actually think that song is also what a black implosion sounds like, think about that next time you listen to it. I used to say all the time that if I had to pick between love and respect, I would pick respect because the human species cannot be trusted with love. Not all the time anyway. We have used (both underused and overused) the word "love" so much that we have dishonored it.

In America, racial identity is synonymous with political identity. Blackness is political in this country. It is harder for some people to humanize pain and joy for Black people because even those two things are seen through racial and political eyes. They cease to be inalienable rights and normal human experiences but rather become a privilege in the eyes of those who are safest to experience them. When you are used to seeing people through a political landscape, it is not easy to see how when a person values things like safety and respect just as you do, that they are worthy of living those things out loud without it being a threat to you.

Respect for me has often been perceived in masculine connotations, similar to Power. Society chooses to assign masculine-associated meanings to Respect and the detrimental implication being that men require respect more than women. Similar to how whiteness has embedded disrespect in how it unfolds itself and the expectation being that blackness can "take it and should take it". Respect accounts for so many catastrophes that have occurred and continue to occur right now regardless of sex, gender, race, etc. No one enjoys being disrespected and no one deserves to be at the receiving end of it.

I am fully aware that Love is who we are, we come from it, and we are it. I am also aware that love, just like respect, has been assigned so-called feminine qualities. The detrimental implication being that men are incapable of acting out of love and that women will deny their self-sovereignty as well as their inherent dignity for 'love.' And well, Saidiya already explains what happens with love in regard to whiteness. Until of course, respect steps into the picture, one of the greatest equalizers to ever exist.

Respect comes in to assist with how to "play the game" as they say. It steps in for those who only know how to cheat or use shortcuts in life. Respect demands that you show up as a human being and walk your way to self-love and loving others healthily, one respectable choice at a time. Respect demands that you put forth the effort it takes to be a present person and not a perfect person- huge difference. However, Respect as beautiful as it is, is seen as a political act, a dangerous ask and hasn't always guaranteed safety for Black people. Even though on a purely human level, it restores dignity even in the seemingly small things.

Love on the other hand, well, the truest kind of Love does not have "rules" per se, it is sufficient unto itself as the great Poet Khalil Gibran says. It chooses you, and if you are willing to follow its path, it guides you and molds you. Love just is, and that type of magic has its place. Respect demands and requires a code of ethics. Unfortunately, even that hasn't always warded off whiteness and all the detrimental ways it exists. As I mentioned earlier, Blackness is often seen through racial and political prisms such that it limits the discussions to an intellectual level. The vastness of Blackness goes beyond mere intellectualization. I decided to talk about respect from a more personal standpoint. I challenge you to sit in that journey with me and choose to connect the dots along the way with me in this essay or later when you think about it more.

It took several seemingly minor moments of disrespect that rippled over into each other and eventually became what I call the "Great Disrespect", for healing to occur in my life. For some of us, it takes one big disaster of disrespect to wake us up; for others, it's recognizing and living out loud the patterns of generational and/or inherited disrespect daily until we get tired of it. Then there is a group of us whose initial introduction to disrespect becomes the defining way we walk this walk called Life. And then for another group of us, it takes multiple "blind moments" of disrespect that creates a slow but delicious grand awareness of it. It all depends on the speed with which we individually learn or are ready to hear the truth.

We all have a story to tell about moments where casual disrespect was thrown around here and there to our faces or behind our backs. In my life, it took someone I thought was a friend to disrespect me in a way that shook my spirit, a spiritual violation of epic proportions that allowed me to come back home to myself. I experienced a heartbreak from a former friend that launched me into a full-on investigation centered on the following questions, "does anybody else see this? This can't be real, right?" or "how did I not see this about this person/situation?". These particular questions are their own brand of torture. They are marred with feelings of regret, shock, disappointment, shame, anger, dismay, confusion, hurt, etc. The head trip you go on and the heartbreak that is experienced during this time needs to feed those questions, so the spiral is insane!

It is because at the core of the many replays that occurred for me, I was trying to heal the wound of self-betrayal directly linked to the ways I allowed disrespect to go unchecked. Furthermore, the price I pay for wearing Black skin because as I said earlier, respect doesn't always ward off whiteness. There really are steep consequences to demanding respect including death for a Black person. For a while, it is as though I existed outside of myself, afraid to trust myself, to listen, or even believe in myself. I was essentially moving between voluntarily vacating my inner Home or evicting myself. Until I finally understood that I was dying to the old Self that had walked me up to that moment of the Great

Disrespect. My observation is that the violation that comes from disrespect feels like a robbery or a house break-in. The analogy of the robbery and/or house break-in can conjure up so many scenarios in peoples' minds so here is what I am choosing to focus on.

When people burglarize someone's home, unless they go for the usual "valuable things" in there, the assumption underneath that criminal act is that whatever it is they took, has value enough for them to use for their own purpose. This is not really about the sentimental value of the item to the person who got robbed, but rather what the burglar thinks they have gained. Similarly, heartbreaks born out of disrespect assume that the deeds performed (both verbal and nonverbal) are warranted. The worst part of the violation is the underlying assumption that the disrespectful person makes. Whether they intended to or not, the disrespect was a direct assault on our sacred Pristine place, the place that belongs to no one else but GOD and you. The space where your most precious jewel lives and houses the truth of WHO you really are.

Have you ever seen the way people treat you when they believe they are more powerful than you, more deserving and entitled to be here than you, when they believe you are not valuable because they are the ones who assign that value on and to you? When they believe your value as a general state of being is theirs to give or take away? And so, I reiterate the title and the main point of this essay. It is almost always about RESPECT. It is absolutely important to know the value you have within a home and as the Home, it's a sign of self-respect.

I purport that the burglar and the disrespectful person share the same prerogative. In the burglar's attempt to "break in or vandalize or harm and/or steal", they not only cause harm by breaking into your home and stealing "your stuff". They intended (consciously or not) to leave the lasting impression that you will never be or feel safe and see value within your own Home ever again. That to me, is the biggest violation of them all. Mama Maya Angelou said that there must always remain within us a place that is pristine, a place that only GOD dwells, a place that we defend with everything in us because it only belongs to GOD and you. That is the Home within us all and knowing this only serves to help us honor, dare I say respect, other people's homes too.

In my culture, there is a common admonition used that loosely translates to, "*Act like you come from somewhere or like you belong somewhere*". This is directly correlated to the sentiment of respecting the Home within yourself and the home we share with others. The burglar and the disrespectful person attempt to harm what is sacred when they "break in". They treat you, your inner Home, that pristine place like it has no value and attempt to make you believe that you do not "come from somewhere or you do not belong somewhere".

This sentiment I know will be felt on a visceral level by those who come from collective cultures, because it just hits differently. Most times when you disrespect an African person, you have dragged their entire family and lineage into that, you have called the ancestors up and out of their graves into that entire disrespectful situation. That is why we get riled up, because the offense wakes up even the dead and buried. When people decide to treat you as though you do not come from somewhere or belong somewhere, the baseline overtone of their treatment towards you is that you're not enough or worth anything. The bigger offense is the underlying assumption that your worth is somehow theirs to determine in the first place.

Disrespect is another form of spiritual violence. When someone dishonors, disregards, and dismisses you, that shit reverberates on a spiritual level. That level of spiritual violence hits you in the space that is sacred, the place that screams "*I do not belong to you, so you do not get to do as you please when you please. Speak to me and handle me as such*". It is so offensive you feel like you want to come out of your skin, like unzipping it and vomiting whatever it is that is in you as well as on you that could make anyone think they can behave as such. It hurts because you can feel the effort someone has taken to un-affirm truths about you that you know deep down are holy.

Disrespecting someone takes effort and a casual, yet inherent form of self-hate (on the part of the offender) that masks itself as entitlement, ownership and ultimately what they believe is Power. Only those who know they have a whole system to back them up and protect them, could ever dare to treat another human being as chattel, as 'body things', as mere nothingness. If you want to see how puny we can get as human beings, watch someone put effort into being disrespectful. If you allow yourself for one moment to get outside of yourself and watch the person performing "The Great Disrespect", like it's a play or something, you get to see one of the greatest displays of fear.

God allowed me this opportunity, several times after this epic disrespectful moment. I am not sure how I can explain this to you friend, but it felt like I was outside of myself. Time seemed to have slowed down quickly enough for me to intuit what was really happening. Instead of reacting, I was given the opportunity to observe my own feelings and choose how to respond. I had the opportunity to befriend my own fear; to grieve for my sovereignty; implement patience; understand what leverage means; practice and master self-regulation; sharpen my mind and my response-time skills; invite wisdom over wanton indignation and best of all, as I learned from it, I was born anew.

I became really tuned in, it became a moment to evolve as a human being and practice compassion towards myself and others. I allowed myself to see the hypocrisy that lives in all of us. We aspire to goodness but most times than not, we act from our ability to cause pain. I saw all the ways in which I could have caused harm in response to this "break-in/vandalization" but instead I sat in the alchemy of it and mothered myself back to self-sovereignty. I allowed myself to feel all I needed to feel in order to gain the strength I needed to recalibrate, rebuild and start anew. That major moment of the "Great Disrespect" was when my unbowed spirit looked at me the way a trainer looks at their boxer from the corner, yelling "Get up!" after they've been knocked down.

GOD introduced me to my arsenal, some tools I didn't even know I had, and others that had received upgrades. In that disillusioned place that I was in, that felt lonely, dark, confusing, and unfair, that felt like death, God and my ancestors all looked at me and lovingly whispered, "Get up Lioness". The whispers felt like a hug, like hard-won redemption, like victory, love, truth, safety and protection. It felt like Self-Respect and so I got up.

I started the true business of cleaning up my Home, reclaiming the safety and worth within it, installing the proper security systems and of course sharpening my boxing acumen. I believe wholeheartedly that knowing that you have a Home to go back to when life knocks you down, knowing that you are not alone and knowing what name to answer to when you are being called to rise up informs you of how you fight. I believe there is a compound effect in knowing and acting from the Home within ourselves and within others. The two work together, symbiotically.

Many wise teachers have taught this message in as many ways as possible because it is that important. Consistently living and creating from this blessed place called Home, has lifetime benefits and rewards. One of the biggest ones is knowing what Respect means and how to wear it. No matter what the burglar or the heartbreaker intended, true success is contingent upon one thing, and that is the power to assign meaning. We get to completely own the journey to rediscovery, reframing, and yes, even releasing any and/or every precept regarding the terms "home" and respect.

    Well my fellow sojourner, may you walk this world understanding that your worth is inherent, that you are holy and sacred. May you believe that you are worthy of love, truth, safety and protection. May you mother yourself back to Respect and father yourself into Love. May you behold Respect and steward this power as it ought to be.

11.

The Power in Reclaiming a Question

Part One - Tell the complete story

Returning to a place of wholeness is being able to ask yourself a question and then endeavoring to tell the complete story. That is what someone I once knew told me as he witnessed me be unfair to myself when I recounted a very traumatic event to him. He stopped me and said, "hey, tell the complete story, one in which you are fair to yourself". It actually stopped me in my tracks, and I have done this very thing ever since. Let us be clear about something first. "Complete" does not always mean being accurate or being right.

"Accurate" in the sense that you can't speak for all parties involved and so there will always be details missing in that regard, that's one factor to consider. The second thing is, because we are human beings, our memory sometimes does indeed fail us, depending on the level of trauma involved, and of course, the specifics do change because of this. Psychology journals on trauma and memory confirm this as well, look it up. Lastly, accuracy is difficult to establish sometimes, unless everything was caught on camera. Even when there are eyewitnesses, we are good at seeing what we want to see, people can and do lie occasionally (again, this depends on each context and trauma).

"Complete", on a personal level, is about recounting as many details as close to "the truth" as possible - both subjectively and objectively. This is hard to do but can be done, if you're willing to befriend the truth and if you desire peace above all else. Doing this without seemingly denying or condoning any unfair things that happened to you as well. Whew! Like I said, this is hard to do but also why I love questions.

I have lived with questions since I was a child, I was curious and I still am. I am committed to the love I have for questions. There is something humbling about the process of asking a question because you are simultaneously admitting to your ignorance whilst being empowered by your ability to be an open learner. It is a constant state of being humbled because asking a question reminds you that you don't know everything, that you don't have to know everything, and even better, that you want to know something. It takes being joyfully courageous to continue to ask anyway. I know many people are plagued with the fear of not knowing. I have suffered at the hands of that same secret fear too at times. A major part of my healing journey has been unlearning how I used to ask questions.

Example: when I was hurt, especially by people close to me, some of the questions I would ask seemed to cause more suffering and pain. Worse still, the questions were aimed at condemning me and they were marred with judgment. Questions like, "Why didn't I see this coming?'; "Why would I let this happen?"; "What is wrong with me?". Oh, and my personal favorites, "What does this say about me?"; "Why this and why now?"; "Am I really that naive, dumb, stupid… [insert all the very mean adjectives you want]?".

It wasn't until I started asking different questions - kinder, empowering, and fair questions, questions that did not vilify me or the other people, that the true path to freedom started being revealed. Instead of asking damning questions, I began to ask the following: "How are you really feeling about this?", "What did you learn?"; "Do you remember warning signs that preceded this moment? If yes, do you remember what you said to dismiss yourself and your intuition? If no, are you ok forgiving that you didn't see this coming?"; "Are you ok forgiving how you reacted or responded?", "Now that you've learned something, are you willing to be better at being vigilant?"; "What do you need to get yourself off this floor and out of this bucket of ice cream and fried chicken?", etc.

The questions were not guilt or shame-inducing anymore and neither did they create stuck energy. They were not about the other person, or about my "wrongness", they were not about good or bad, sometimes they weren't even about fairness. They were about support, they were about getting angry enough to change, they were about meeting my own immediate needs, about kindness, efficacy in truth-telling, and forward movement - no matter how small the question and/or gesture was that I asked and showed myself, I RESPECTED myself enough to do it.

Reclaiming the power in a question involves knowing when to use the three magical words, "I don't know" and/or "I didn't know" without feeling bad or wrong about oneself.

These words anchored me in moments when fear threatened to stifle and silence me. Questions (when done right) are delicious morsels of GOD's mercy and goodness, they are redemptive and empowering, they are radical and poetic. Reclaiming the power in asking questions invites wisdom, invites humility, and most importantly invites GOD to continue to light the path. Questions have assisted me in being able to move forward and upward in my journey of healing because so much of what I ask now, I don't always get the answers that I want. And even when I do receive some answers, there is still more that is left unanswered. But when I do ask, there is confidence upon confidence that is made manifest almost instantaneously within me.

    The power of asking a question stopped being about reaching for satisfaction or an end to the pain, but rather about the acceptance of what is. It stopped being about reaching forth to get something and became more about grounding myself in what feels good to me, what is just and truthful to each moment. It became about telling the complete story in a way that allowed me to see myself and truly respect myself. Reclaiming the power in asking a question made truth my best friend. Let part two of this essay walk you through another one of those profound questions I was once asked.

Part Two - "Who told you that?"

"Burden of proof" is a legal term I have heard repeatedly because of all the legal shows I love to watch. As it has been with some of my other essays, I heard this term during one of my meditative walks as a potential topic to explore and it stuck with me, so here we are. I am using this terminology for allegorical purposes only. So, I decided to go with the Google definition of the term 'burden of proof' and it is defined as, *"the standard that a party seeking to prove a fact in court must satisfy to have that fact legally established."*

I don't know about you but sometimes the battles in my head sound like a court proceeding, and they are not always civil. The pattern I noticed as I was healing was the unbalanced nature of my conversations with myself. The voices tended to lean towards a certain perception, often false and sometimes unfounded. I didn't allow myself to have better representation when it came to self-analysis you know. Lesson learned: How I structure/frame questions matters deeply. Even more importantly, rooting for myself to win really matters.

The energetic imprint found in questions is both magical and damning, hence they must be honored as well as handled with care, precision, and dexterity. In this 'case', the questions I asked myself directed my attention toward my inherent worthiness and not imposed inadequacy. They pointed me towards disproving the illusions and choosing to surrender the need to prove myself to anyone. The questions beckoned me to change my focus and satisfy the requirements needed for stewardship of Self and consequently of others. They led me to my truest North, inspired me to demystify certain facts, and parcel out what is real from what is fictitious or inconclusive. These questions established a new standard of knowing myself and led me to a place where I could state, unequivocally, that I am loved by me and by GOD.

Along this healing journey, I have met wonderful humans too, people who have asked me provocative and ultimately liberating questions. One such seemingly simple question is as follows: ***Who told you that?*** This question was asked of me in the middle of a rant once by one of these wonderful humans. This question helped short-circuit my brain, which was of tremendous help. I actually stopped mid-rant and realized that most of what I was saying in that moment was regurgitation, a concoction of half-truths and hidden lies, stuff I hadn't taken the time to look through as an adult woman. It kind of reminded me of the way diligent and efficient lawyers sift through evidence to make their cases. It is necessary for us to take that kind of care with these questions especially because the illusions are pervasive and therefore cause several implosions.

What I enjoy about healing and the growth that blossoms from it, is how I now know how to defend myself against my lesser selves (the parts I am working to heal). I am better at self-defense, which is not the same as being defensive. I started to be balanced and fair with myself. ***Who told you that?*** I would ask repeatedly. Four innocuous words, that are wrapped with the Power to free ourselves and to assess the evidence before us so we can discern with graceful grit and get the clarity needed to move forward. It became glaringly clear to me that the two sides to this question possessed two outcomes. One side offered the gifts of edification and empowerment whilst the other intended to keep its prisoners shackled and stuck in self-flagellation because they were beholden to unworthiness.

The excavation into my past selves felt like a court in session at times, where the burden of proof lay in the hands of my past selves to provide evidence of my supposed unworthiness. It got messy, murky, and even mean. The past selves wanted to continually bring up all the things that burdened me and lay them at my feet as established facts. Healing requires that I let go and want something more than the pain, more than being right and more than being afraid of being seen as weak. Once I wanted my healing more than being right or being "innocent/good", I no longer needed to own any guilt, shame, etc., I wanted redemption. I wanted to be free of this bullshit. The power dynamics shifted, and it dawned on me then, that it was not on me to "prove" anything to anyone, including my past selves too. The burden of proof did not belong to me.

Walking courageously through this journey of healing has looked like dropping every heavy thing I carried and prioritizing Me. That includes being able to "hold court" within myself and endeavor to see through all the muck I would be combing through. When you believe you are worthy, this act of self-love as well as self-respect anchors you and is no longer intimidating or daunting. Because when I started fretting over myself, knowing I mattered, how I talked to myself changed drastically. I stopped mislabeling my feelings, which is a big one to be mindful of, because making sure what you feel is actually what you feel, matters. I stopped thinking that I was a burden or that this kind of healing work was burdensome. It became a pleasure to seek and create my own standard of things like peace and joy. No debate, no delays, no distractions, no rush, no doubt or questioning it - just action upfront. And knowing I'm fully worthy of that kind of attention felt glorious.

Frantz Fanon, who I have mentioned a lot already, was a big fan of rebuilding oneself through releasing the 'false sense of Self'. The context here is: Fanon was focused on decolonizing the mind and ultimately society as a whole. He strongly believed that through education and collective awareness, we would be able to achieve freedom. But he also pointed out a main caveat which was that, first, the rebuilding must start within each individual. He strongly emphasized that freedom was tied to releasing that false sense of Self that was built through exploitation from others. Once we addressed that part of ourselves that was in bondage, we could truly rebuild our minds and ultimately nations.

He also made sure to emphasize that the process can and will be violent, not just physically but also emotionally, spiritually and mentally. This process is hard. It requires ongoing commitment and a healthy relationship with discomfort. Fanon's vision is something I harken to, as I rebuild and reclaim my path to self-sovereignty through the questions I ask. I desire a more compassionate and kinder way of analyzing my thoughts and feelings so as to see myself clearly, see my path clearly, and as a result see others clearly.

Here is where I am now whenever I "hold court" within my moments of reflection. I require top notch representation every time I hold court within myself. I lead the proceedings with love, respect, safety, truth and protection. The standard I create for myself includes removing derogatory remarks on my spiritual reputation and replacing them with what the ancestors call me. They call me an answered prayer; a born free; an heiress apparent to the wealth they established for me; a Lioness! I answer to those names. I replace the derogatory remarks with GOD's evident love for me. I seek to empower myself by demystifying certain facts and establishing a new way of executing my belief in myself.

Whatever you choose, fellow sojourner, I hope you defend yourself with respect and graceful grit, your truest Self deserves that kind of representation.

EPILOGUE

"The day I saw Her"

I created a written series titled "*The day I saw Her*" and in this series, I celebrate the women who have fortified me during this healing expedition. I write about each woman and the lessons she has taught me. Engaging with these lessons felt like a lovely unfurling of feminine power (the light and the dark of it). I had the opportunity to be enveloped in this glorious feeling of being mothered, of companionship and of being steeped in healing power. I am grateful.

The title of this book is called *"Unzip My Skin"* and I have decided to end this book with three specific ancestors. They chose to unzip their skins in their own ways and gave us the very best of themselves. Their specific and unique imprint in how they chose to live life was my guiding light. My true business as I am healing is to be inspired, to learn from and with my ancestors, to be edified and fortified by them. My true business is to sit down and listen, to pivot and to accept, and to no longer abandon myself when I make mistakes. These black implosions I have shared with you are representations of a soul that has accepted love and was liberated because of it. I honor them and the unbowed spirit that sprung forth because of my writing journey. I end this book with lessons from my Gogo (grandmother), Mama Maya Angelou and the Zimbabwean Legend, Mbuya Nehanda.

Mbuya Nehanda

I really didn't enjoy history when I was in high school. This wasn't because I disliked the teacher, but the moment I understood that the history books I was using had not been fully decolonized, it irked me to "study" history. We still had to adhere to a "colonial truth" so I really didn't feel like I could pay attention nor aspire to 'pass' a class that was teaching half-truths and whole lies. Needless to say, I didn't pass this class (lol). I wasn't happy about the grade I got and the way it looked on my report card at the time. But I looked at it again as an adult woman and I can honestly say, I felt ok about it. What I enjoyed the most about history was in grade school actually, because I learned about some of the most prominent Zimbabwean historical figures. Most of the figures that were highlighted were men of course (insert a Black girl eye roll right here please!). But the few brilliant women mentioned stayed with me including this one legend named Mbuya Nehanda.

The few women that were talked about, extensively and not just as footnotes, fascinated me. I heard about Mbuya Nehanda in grade school, she read like a myth and a legend. Gosh, this woman haunted me, but in the best way. Here is the general gist about her, but I suggest you go look her up for yourself as she is an incredible ancestor. She was mainly known for her role as a spiritual leader during the resistance against British colonial rule in Zimbabwe. Her spiritual leadership role was as a spirit medium, but not in the mainstream and demonized sense that we have come to know. She was seen as a connection to the ancestors and from this connection, war strategies were created to assist in fighting against the British colonizers. "*Mhondoro*", is what they call individuals like her, a powerful and ancestral spirit that speaks through a human who is the conduit.

One of the main strategies to win against British colonial rule during this phase of the Chimurenga (there were three phases) was centered on Zimbabwean spirituality. Before colonization, Zimbabweans understood their relationship to the God of their traditional religion sometimes known as *Mwari*. My dad used to say, "*Musikavanhu*" as the other name for God, which translates to the "Creator of People/All". Each tribe had their own traditional spiritual practices. Under Mbuya Nehanda's leadership, they almost steered British colonizers off, but they did not have enough military supplies in the end to defeat them.

The key part I remember about Mbuya Nehanda though, was the stance she took before she was hanged. She was tried and found guilty of killing British soldiers, and before she was hanged, she refused to convert to Christianity and announced that she would return and rise up again until Zimbabwe was free. Sheesh! I remember re-reading this story about her as a grown woman and being in utter admiration of that kind of Power. This woman's dying words were that her bones and spirit would rise again to finish what she started.

That particular act of power and defiance she showed at that moment haunted me. Her last words haunted me. And she came back to mind as I was exploring and learning about my implosions. Much of why I wanted healing above the suffering was because humans like this woman existed (and more exist in the present too). I stand firmly in my power as a woman and as an African when I am centered in my identity as a spiritual person like she did.

Christianity as well as Zimbabwean traditional spirituality are in some ways still intrinsically tied to how I have chosen to heal. I used to be conflicted about this because I could hear the cries of my ancestors, weeping over the constant spiritual violence Afro peoples inflict upon ourselves when we blatantly dismiss and deny our African spiritual identities. But that dissonance has since dissipated within me because I do not deny or dismiss my spiritual identity. I am a Lioness, through and through. What Mbuya Nehanda did for me was give me a backbone, a fort to stand on and behind, a spiritual blueprint of sorts.

She was a great strategist, a great warrior, a great leader. And it all stemmed from her standing as a conduit, a great spiritual leader who was tapped in and focused on what I call the cauldron of Afro/Zimbabwean essence. Her triumph and power are my inheritance! The day I saw Her, Mbuya Nehanda, is the day I received ancestral grit which would lead me back to myself. The soul whispers that come from this woman are marred with all the scars we wear as Afro descendants, but also all the glory. That dissonance that came with colonialism and slavery threatened to immerse us in the illusions of separateness, unconnected to both our true Self and to each other as Afro descendants. The inheritance she left me (left us) in her final words, that her bones and spirit would rise again to finish what she started, are made manifest every time I choose self-sovereignty. Whilst others may choose to only hear violence in her words or to diminish the spiritual power she possessed, what I behold is a continuity of self-sovereignty echoing through time.

The unconquerable soul that exists in my tribal identity as a Lioness chooses freedom always. Mbuya Nehanda made a choice that day to respond not to what the British named her, but to what her ancestors called her. They called her a warrior spirit and she made a choice that day that reverberated generations later. I am not concerned about the conflict some Africans still carry within them about what to believe in, Christianity vs. "demon worship" a.k.a African traditional spirituality. [**Sidenote**: yes, there are people who genuinely use

African/Zimbabwean spiritual practices for evil, Christians do the same with their own theology]. I was able to go through all the seemingly conflicting information and found that focusing on evolving as a spiritual being versus performative spirituality served my soul immensely. As it is with all things hypocrisy, I have lived long enough to see how we can easily be misled by wanting to prove to one another that we are something that we are not.

My true business has been to focus on the "becoming" - on BEING my true Self. My true business is about my ever-evolving soul and not on the salesmanship of what theology is better than the other. I remain aware of dark entities all the time, for they are dressed in every skin color, theology, financial status, manufactured personalities, etc., there is on this planet. Embodying my spiritual identity through my tribal totem helped me see past many limited as well as distorted beliefs and I shall remain focused on that above all else.

All other forms of identity either kept me hostage, would try to extort me, ask me to betray myself, and would promote hypocrisy and imbalance in exchange for temporary freedoms. It all felt like a gimmick to keep me focused on anything but the truth of who I am. What I hear every time I think of and speak of Mbuya Nehanda is the unbowed spirit, the Lion spirit, an Afro essence that lives beyond time. One that all African children can call on and can choose to answer to. I hear her and the rest of the ancestors telling us to hold on to our Respect and Pride, to embody love and befriend truth. To establish safety in all things and to protect our homes. To ultimately embody a form of Power that transcends our baser and often hypocritical natures. I hope for Afro descendants to choose the path of the gloriously unbowed.

Ndatenda (thank you) Mbuya Nehanda for showing a fearless and gritty way to exist in this world.

Mama Maya Angelou

"*Love liberates*" - that is what Maya Angelou said. I have a tattoo of those exact words spoken by this woman. When I say her essence is "written" on me, I mean both figuratively and literally. I wear it gracefully. Mama Maya's voice is one of the ever-loving echoes that guides me in specific ways, especially as I write. She is an ancestor that I looked to and whose journey seemed to speak to me the most. But please allow me to honor other American ancestors I leaned on as well. I honor bell hooks, Alice Walker, Toni

Morrison, Audre Lorde, and a bevy of many other prolific Black American women writers. Thank you all for the love letters you gave us, and because I am a writer, I have an idea of what it takes to put these words on paper. I salute you.

Mama Maya said that my crown was bought and paid for, and after I read those words, I chose to stand on that wisdom daily. At my most challenging moments, I repeat those words to myself so I can always remember that a price had been paid for my freedom. By both the ancestors on the continent and in the diaspora. I must also add that I grew up being repeatedly told about how my Zimbabwean ancestors fought against British rule so I could be free. '*Born free*' that is what they called the generation born after Zimbabwean independence in 1980. I think that constant reminder combined with my healing journey emphasized why freedom is at the forefront of my mind quite often.

There are so many ways to say something, that has the main reason why I loved literature for as long as I have. And it's why I loved Mama Maya's work. I enjoy the process of being able to look at something and see the many ways I can express it and interpret it. Words are powerful for this very reason. One carefully crafted sentence could become the anthem for destruction or restoration. Mama Maya's words restore me continually. The words of our ancestors - the ones that went unspoken, that were erased, muffled and stifled, the words that were forcefully taken, twisted and perverted. Mama Maya found a way to transmit those words back to us so we could hear them and wear the grace in them once again.

I behold her work because she simultaneously sounded like she was weeping and roaring through her work. *"Love liberates"*, is what she said when she was explaining what love means to her. I have harkened to this belief during my healing walk, and I am anchored by this because it opens up the scope of what freedom means. It continually gives the power back to me but extends the conversation outward - a symbiotic experience once again. What I imagined about freedom entailed all things masculine - the aggression, the fight, the grit, the sacrifice, etc., and that is a part of it. Mama Maya's work helped expand on the meaning of liberation and taught me the grace within *Why the Caged Bird Sings*.

She taught me to listen, to really listen, because the hard part was already done. My crown had been bought and paid for, so not all suffering was necessary, and not all sacrifice was mine to make anymore. I hear her voice when I am surrounded by books, even if I am sitting in silence in a library or in my Home. The pristine place I spend time with GOD, looks like a library where I have access to so much sacred knowledge and conversations with sojourners such as Mama Maya. The thought itself makes me giddy! Mama Maya comes to me in moments when I need to remember the importance of stewardship, especially regarding the Pristine place. She awakens in me the fire that makes me want to rise, day by day, and love myself as well as others. And I am grateful for and to her.

Ndatenda (thank you) Mama Maya. I will adorn my unbowed Crown, gracefully.

Embracing a fellow Lioness' Wisdom

Yup! My Gogo (or grandmother - maternal grandmother) is also a Lioness. If you remember, I said before that a child's identity within my culture is patrilineal therefore, because her father came from a different Lion tribe than mine, she is a Masivanda as well. My patrilineal grandmother, my dad's mother, was also a Lioness. I actually found out that my matrilineal great grandmother was a Lioness, also. Needless to say, (but I will anyway), I have the power of the Lion DEEP within my spiritual DNA.

This full circle moment is how I chose to end this book. I enjoyed writing it for this very reason because there are so many ways I got reintroduced to myself, and this was also an opportunity to talk about the only grandmother I actually had the privilege of knowing while she was living. My Gogo, my beloved grandmother, passed away in 2018. She was a Jesus-loving, laughter-filled, free-spirited dancer and joy-spreader. The way I remember my grandmother is rather self-serving though. Because of my interpretation of how she walked this journey called life, I saw her as a free spirit. The free spirit in me as a kid wanted a friend who understood me, and that was my Gogo in some ways.

There are aspects of Her that will forever be badass in my eyes, even though I did not get a chance to know her as a woman - to really hear her life story and not the mythological creature I had made her out to be in my mind or the profound elder she was in our family. I would have loved to know Her as Theresa, the girl who became a woman. Gogo shared some stories about her life here and there, and I would hear stories about her from her own children as well. But they were small pieces of the grand, as well as a beautiful puzzle that she was. Regrettably, not only did I not get to spend as much time as I would have liked with my Gogo when I was a child, but I wasn't there before she died as well. However, in the moments

I did spend with her, the ones I remember, she would often say these things that at the time I thought were crazy, and also way too deep for my young child's mind to grasp. And yet as they say, she planted a seed. After she passed, she would come to me all the time with reminders that would tug at my heart incessantly, whether in my dreams or as "random" thoughts and songs. These memories I carry are of the things she once said that I rolled my eyes at but are now my saving grace. I want to share a couple of them with you, in memory of my Gogo. I call them my Gogo-isms.

The **first Gogo-ism** has to do with self-love and self-care. I was around 10 or 11 years old when my Gogo was visiting us in the city in Zimbabwe. She was a farm girl who rarely liked city life. On this day, I ran out of the shower, quickly put lotion on my body, and was about to rush out of the room when she stopped me in the typical Gogo fashion, with a spoonful of disrespect (lol). She sat me down and asked me, "*Nhai iwe* (hey you), whose body is this?". I was baffled and incensed because I had places to be, and she was about to lecture me as usual. So I answered, "Mine," and she asked me again, the same question. I repeated, "Mine," only now with a more subdued agitation. She responded, "Exactly," and I thought, "Oook…?" (insert an internal eye roll right here because I would never dare to do that in actual real-time; she would have spanked me).

She sat me down and walked me through a couple of scars on her body, and stories about those scars. She showed me her wrinkles, features she didn't particularly like on her body, and some of her favorite marks on her body, and then she said, "Do you know how and why I remember all this about myself?". She explained that her body was hers, so when she put lotion on her body or took time while showering, it was a moment of celebration and recognition of the body that belonged to her. To see all the scars and wrinkles that reminded her not only of her mortality but of the body she had been given. To remember its sanctity as a gift from God.

She emphasized that this wasn't a duty performed for man's pleasure but a sacred engagement between her and God. Everything else was a by-product. As I now walk this journey of self-care and self-love, stewardship continues to make itself known to me. As I take care of my body, I am reminded of how crucial "body care" is to holistic healing. I now see the profundity of what she meant, that this body is to be honored for the purpose it serves in our human journey. We often talk a lot about our purpose on earth as humans, but we do not think that our physical bodies too have their own purpose. Maybe some of us do, but we as humans have created a hierarchy of purpose that often puts the body last. Our bodies carry us, they house our vital organs which are imperative to our wellbeing, and they protect as well as provide for us. What a deep purpose this body has, one that needs our cooperation. Our bodies deserve all the time in the world to be loved like my Gogo did with hers (presence, not perfection, remember that). So, get to it and love yourself in the ways only you can.

Here is **another Gogo-ism**. As always, Gogo would catch me mid-stride because she couldn't help herself. Truth be told, my nickname was "speedy" after all, so there was no other way to catch me but mid-stride. She dropped this gem on me as I was rushing to get out the door yet again. She said, "Do you know when you were born, you were already beginning to die." Of course, I was like, "Ook...," which was my typical response at this point. You might have heard of this by now, thanks to the movie the Black Panther. In most African cultures, our relationship with death isn't linear; it is fluid and cyclical. I did not understand this at the time though but the idea of death, of talking about death is not strange to me. Hence, my relationship with death was and is not a scary one. I was more concerned about how I was going to die and not if or when I was going to die.

Gogo explained that death is a beautiful part of life. This lesson stuck with me in different ways, and I think in some ways that I always knew as a child. I think that's why I was so interested in experiencing as much as I could, as joyfully as I could with an innocent-like urgency. Because the urgency and agency with which life is meant to be lived is the gratitude we show to God for the time given on Earth. Death becomes a welcomed stage in life, because it really isn't the end. It is not necessarily what we do in life, but how we do Life. Mama Maya Angelou encouraged us all to live life with style and pizzazz, whatever that means to you. I plan on living this life just as she advised. What about you?

This is **the last of the Gogo-isms** I will share with you. My Gogo once asked me, "Do you know why your heart, brain, and soul aren't outside of your body?" I remember squinting my eyes in confusion because, as you may have noticed, a Zimbabwean grandmother cannot teach a lesson without an elaborate metaphor or anecdote. However, this time, the lesson was short, and I don't know if she was tired or if it was intentional, or both. She asked the question and gave me a brief but potent answer. She explained that "if the mind, heart, and soul were meant to exist outside of this body, God would have created different 'houses' to hold them all. And yet, in all of

God's infinite wisdom, all three are housed in one place, which is this body." She chuckled and said, "Well, I suppose God also accounted for the fact that we can be a lazy creation; we can barely take care of this one house, so three would have been a disaster," That was it, she said what she said, and she kept on laughing about it and walked off.

And I, as I have already shown, quietly left the conversation thinking, "Ooookk…" That was the end of that lesson. After having had my own time on this earth, experiencing miracles and making enough life-altering 'mistakes', I hear her words loud and clear now. Thanks to my Gogo this healing journey has been guided by her wisdom. There is no healing without letting all parts of me engage as the collaborators that they are. My heart, mind, body and soul invited each other into a collaborative journey of walking me back Home to myself. I understood that each collaborator has their own speed and way of processing joy as well as trauma.

It was my duty and honor to steward this and invite inner partnership instead of succumbing to the frustration, confusion and impatience that comes with "knowing thyself". I needed to liberate myself from myself. And to do that I also needed to be aware of my nihilistic tendencies. With Gogo's help, through her whispers of Lioness wisdom, I was able to do so with graceful grit.

Ndatenda hangu Masi (thank you Lioness), for all your wisdom. I'll be listening out for more of your joyful and laughter-filled whispers, Gogo.

Acknowledgements

This book is evidence that I am a well-loved woman. I have been blessed with wonderful human beings and human experiences, all of which I learned a great deal from. I thank my family, both blood and chosen, for how wide my wings keep growing because of your love for me.

To my ancestors, whose presence through my totem as a Lioness has both shielded and catapulted me into an expression of power that is my own to embrace and share, ndatenda (thank you).

And to you the reader, thank you so much for taking the time to engage with my work and allowing your curious nature to prevail. May you behold the kind of love that calls the glory of the unbowed spirit out of yourself. May you also live out your expression of power in this life.

Yours truly - The Lioness.

Works cited

Fanon, Frantz. *Black Skin, White Masks*. Grove Press, 2008.

Fanon, Frantz. *The Wretched of the Earth*. Translated by Richard Philcox, Grove Press, 2004.

Hartman, Saidiya. *Lose Your Mother: A Journey Along the Atlantic Slave Route*. Farrar, Straus and Giroux, 2007.

Baszile, Jennifer. *The Black Girl Next Door: A Memoir*. Simon & Schuster, 2009.

Freire, Paulo. *Pedagogy of the Oppressed*. Translated by Myra Bergman Ramos, Bloomsbury Academic, 2000.

Soyinka, Wole. "The Fourth Stage." *Myth, Literature, and the African World*. Cambridge University Press, 1976, pp. 26–45.

Soyinka, Wole. "Neo-Tarzanism: The Poetics of Pseudo-Tradition." *Myth, Literature and the African World*, Cambridge University Press, 1976, pp. 47-60.

DeGruy, Joy. *Post Traumatic Slave Syndrome: America's Legacy of Enduring Injury and Healing*. Joy DeGruy Publications, 2005.

Mbembe, Achille. *Necropolitics*. Translated by Steven Corcoran, Duke University Press, 2019.

Mbembe, Achille. "Bodies as Borders." *FES Journal of Political Economy*, vol. 1, no. 1, 2021, pp. 14-26.

Lost:
"Definition of Lost." *Google*, Google, 30 Dec. 2024, www.google.com/search?q=lost.

Burden of Proof:
"Definition of Burden of Proof." *Google*, Google, 30 Dec. 2024, www.google.com/search?q=burden+of+proof.